D0953591

At Issue

Performance
Enhancing Drugs

Other Books in the At Issue Series:

At Issue

Performance Enhancing Drugs

Louise Gerdes, Book Editor

GREENHAVEN PRESS
A part of Gale, Cengage Learning

GALE
CENGAGE Learning™

Detroit • New York • San Francisco • New Haven, Conn • Waterville, Maine • London

Christine Nasso, *Publisher*
Elizabeth Des Chenes, *Managing Editor*

© 2008 Greenhaven Press, a part of Gale, Cengage Learning.

For more information, contact:
Greenhaven Press
27500 Drake Rd.
Farmington Hills, MI 48331-3535
Or you can visit our Internet site at gale.cengage.com

LIBRARY OF CONGRESS CATALOGING-IN-PUBLICATION DATA

Performance enhancing drugs / Louise Gerdes, book editor.
    p. cm. -- (At issue)
  Includes bibliographical references and index.
  ISBN-13: 978-0-7377-3693-9 (hardcover)
  ISBN-10: 0-7377-3693-3 (hardcover)
  ISBN-13: 978-0-7377-3694-6 (pbk.)
  ISBN-10: 0-7377-3694-1 (pbk.)
  1. Doping in sports. 2. Steroids. I. Gerdes, Louise I., 1953-
  RC1230.P476 2007
  362.29--dc22

                                                            2007032384

Printed in the United States of America
2 3 4 5 6 7 12 11 10 09 08

Contents

Introduction

Home-run hitter Mark McGwire ended his career in 2001 with 583 home runs, a record that ranks seventh in baseball history. He had hit 50 or more home runs four seasons in a row from 1996 to 1999. Nevertheless, on his first nomination in 2007, American sportswriters did not elect McGwire to the Baseball Hall of Fame. He received only 128 of the 545 votes cast. Many speculate that sports writers failed to select McGwire due to his connection with baseball's steroid scandal and what many saw as his failure to cooperate with the investigation. On March 17, 2005, McGwire explained his reluctance before the House Government Reform Committee: "Asking me or any other player to answer questions about who took steroids in front of television cameras will not solve the problem. If a player answers 'No,' he simply will not be believed; if he answers 'Yes,' he risks public scorn and endless government investigations." McGwire's silence, however, was not enough to shield him from scorn. His guilt by association with the steroid scandal was, in the eyes of many, the reason he was not inducted into the hallowed hall of fame.

Between 1997 and 2007, sports commentators began to question the meaning of modern sports records and the place modern sports heroes should have in history. Speculation that many of the heroes of modern American baseball have used performance-enhancing drugs has for many tainted the sport. One debate in the controversy over performance-enhancing drugs and whether these drugs threaten American sport concerns the role sports plays in American culture. Some claim that sports in the United States, particularly professional sports, are purely consumer entertainment. These commentators claim that performance-enhancing drugs are, right or wrong, simply another strategy to improve performance and, in turn, increase ticket sales. Others argue that sports are more than entertainment; sports figures are cultural heroes.

Of those who see sports as a reflection of culture, some look back nostalgically on baseball's unenhanced heroes as an example. "For many Americans," asserts professor Danny Duncan Collum, "major league baseball was once the theater in which our social dramas were acted out, and the place we looked for heroes—those people who could tell us what might be possible for free people in a democratic culture." Collum points to Babe Ruth, who made 714 career home runs "on a diet consisting mostly of Prohibition booze, cheap hot dogs, and an impoverished orphan's insatiable need for love and acceptance." Collum also points to the record-breaking career of Hank Aaron, who he claims was fueled by suppressed rage at racism. Collum said, "When Aaron hit number 715, in Atlanta, of all places, many of America's pre-Jackie Robinson wrongs were symbolically righted."

While some lament the loss of less ambiguous sports heroes—imperfect men who combined hard work and genetic gifts to reach superhuman goals, these analysts nevertheless see performance enhancement in sports as inevitable. "Heroism tacitly entails the presence of some force greater than human choice. Human heroes must be or must seem to be more-than-human," observes technology writer Douglas Kern. Indeed, he reasons, performance-enhancing drugs and the enhancements that will inevitably follow may forever change what it means to be a sports hero. "Designing the latest performance-enhancing drugs," Kern claims, "is perhaps a new kind of heroism—an example of the transcendent greatness of man-the-engineer. But this is heroism of a very different sort: It is less available to ordinary human experience; it is less inspiring of the noble human passions; it is more premeditated and less majestic." While future baseball players will run faster and hit the ball farther and more often, many will not see these heroes in the same way. "We will look back to yesterday's heroes, with their bad genes, with their unsuppressed fear and unenhanced intellects and untreated maladies," Kern concludes, "and we will wonder to ourselves: 'How did they do it?' And we will reclaim our wisdom and our humanity when we rediscover the answer."

Some who mourn the loss of yesterday's baseball heroes argue that sports figures who use performance-enhancing drugs expose flaws in American culture. These commentators claim that performance-enhancing drugs reflect the often erroneous contemporary American attitude that bigger and faster are better. Sports writer Dan O'Neill writes: "Performance-enhancing drugs are consistent with the American way. In today's society, we are all about making things better and more expedient." O'Neill's cynicism is evident when he compares the self-improvement of cosmetic surgery to the performance-enhancement of professional baseball players. "So you're old and just can't stand the look of those wrinkles in the corner of your eyes. What do you do? You inject botox into your face and get rid of those nasty and repulsive wrinkles! What's the difference," O'Neill asks, "between shooting collagen into your face and [home-run hitter] Jose Conseco shooting steroids into Mark McGwire's ass? I can't differentiate between the two."

Other observers assert that despite the steroid scandal, sports fans continue to flock to watch enhanced athletes. Right or wrong, these analysts argue, professional sports are guided by massive sports entertainment dynasties competing for consumer dollars. Performance-enhancing drugs, they maintain, produce athletes that provide an exciting spectacle for American consumers. In 2006, despite the steroid scandal, the combined attendance of all thirty major league teams topped 76 million. "Evidence does not support the claim that fans care greatly about which practices athletes use, or that public interest in—or appreciation of—sports will be diminished if athletes try to enhance their performance," maintains Norman

Fost, steroids' biggest defender. "Spectator interest in almost all sports has remained steadfast," he asserts, "notwithstanding widespread and growing awareness of the use of science's numerous enhancements." Indeed, Fost points out, what drew many fans to baseball in the late 1990s was the home-run battle between Sammy Sosa and Mark McGwire.

When sports writers denied McGwire's induction into the Baseball Hall of Fame in 2007, debates over his worthiness erupted in the media. The controversy over the impact of performance-enhancing drugs on professional and amateur sports continues. Indeed, no major sporting event or record pursuit seems immune to debate over the influence of performance-enhancing drugs. The authors in *At Issue: Performance Enhancing Drugs* join the debate, expressing their views on the nature and scope of performance-enhancing drugs and the policies that will best protect athletes and the integrity of sports.

1

Performance-Enhancing Drugs: An Overview

Kenneth Jost

Kenneth Jost, an adjunct professor at Georgetown University Law Center, is a regular contributor to CQ Researcher *and author of* Supreme Court Yearbook.

The use of performance-enhancing drugs in sport generates heated debate. Those who oppose their use claim that these drugs are bad for sports and pose a health risk to athletes who use them. These anti-doping advocates support strict testing protocols, and some call for lifetime bans for those caught using performance-enhancing drugs. Those who oppose these strict policies argue that lifetime bans are an overreaction to exaggerated claims against performance-enhancing drugs. Moreover, strict doping policy critics maintain that test results are sometimes inaccurate, and testing can easily be circumvented by the use of new hard-to-detect drugs.

Drugs have become a major part of elite athletic competition. A significant but unknown number of Olympic hopefuls in the United States and elsewhere, as well as many collegiate and other professional athletes, use chemical substances to increase strength and stamina beyond what they can achieve by nutrition and training alone.

"It's human nature to obtain an edge, whether in combat, in business or in sports," says Charles Yesalis, a professor of health and human development at Pennsylvania State University and a leading expert on—and opponent of—performance-enhancing drugs.

Through the years, athletes have sought that edge from a variety of stimulants ranging from caffeine and brandy to heroin and cocaine. But the isolation of the male hormone testosterone in the 1930s paved the way for more sophisticated chemical agents known as anabolic ("tissue-building") steroids.

The Use of Steroids

Steroids produce masculinizing effects comparable to those from naturally occurring testosterone. The resulting increase in muscle mass may be a boon for weightlifters, football players, or athletes in track and field throwing events. But steroids also produce undesirable side effects. Some, such as acne and increased body hair, are largely cosmetic. Others are more serious, including tumors and cancer in the liver, increased cholesterol levels and—in some men—shrunken testicles. Women who use steroids see many of the same effects, along with a deeper voice and—in some cases—an enlarged clitoris.

As the monetary and other rewards of elite competition have increased over the years, steroids have tempted many ranking athletes.

However, the medical effects of steroids are not fully researched, and some athletes and a handful of vocal critics of anti-drug enforcement efforts in sports dispute the health risks claimed by opponents or say they can be minimized. But their use in athletic competition has been widely viewed as unseemly at best ever since the practice first came to widespread attention in the 1960s.

Nonetheless, as the monetary and other rewards of elite competition have increased over the years, steroids have tempted many top-ranking athletes. "The pressure on people to try different things is very high," says William Roberts, an associate professor at the University of Minnesota's St. John's Hospital and president of the American College of Sports Medicine. "The difference between first and fifth place is the difference between fame and money and relative anonymity."

The Anti-Doping Code

National and international sports federations and professional sports leagues were slow to respond to mounting evidence that steroid use has been increasing since the 1970s. In 1999, however, an international conference of governments and sports organizations led to the writing of a world "anti-doping" code that calls for a two-year suspension in most cases for athletes found to have used banned drugs. The conference also led to the creation of the independent World Anti-Doping Agency (WADA) to police the practice in international competitions, including the Olympics. [The term "doping" has been used to denote use of performance-enhancing drugs in sports at least since the 1930s. Some critics of anti-doping policies maintain the term is inherently pejorative and improperly skews the debate over the issue.]

The [July 2004] charges against [Olympic runner Tim] Montgomery and other U.S. track stars [were] brought by WADA's counterpart in the United States: the U.S. Anti-Doping Agency (USADA). . . .

The evidence against the athletes . . . appears to come from business records seized in a September 2003 raid by federal and state authorities on a San Francisco-area sports lab, the Bay Area Laboratory Cooperative (BALCO), run by sports nutritionist Victor Conte. Federal authorities acted after USADA tipped them off to the existence of a new so-called designer drug—tetrahydrogestrinone or THG—similar to previously known steroids but altered slightly to avoid detection.

USADA itself had been tipped off by a then-unidentified track coach, who sent the anti-doping agency a syringe in June [2003] containing the new steroid and named Conte as the source. Conte's past clients include [Barry] Bonds, who has tried unsuccessfully to dispel suspicions that his bulked-up physique and increased home run output in recent years are signs of steroid use.

Anti-doping officials acknowledge they face an uphill battle in trying to stay ahead of pharmacological advances.

Under Pressure

The raids touched off a succession of high-profile events, including testimony before a federal grand jury by Bonds and many other well-known athletes and an eventual indictment of Conte and three others announced on Feb. 12 [2004] by Attorney General John Ashcroft. "This is not just a call to action," Ashcroft said. "It is a call to the values that make our nation and its people strong and free."

Even before the BALCO investigation, Major League Baseball (MLB) was under pressure to more vigorously curb what several players publicly described as widespread use of steroids. President Bush added to the pressure in his State of the Union address on Jan. 20 [2004] by calling on "football, baseball and other sports" to "get rid of steroids now."

For years, the Major League Baseball Players Association had resisted drug testing, but the union agreed in 2002 to a year of anonymous random tests. If more than 5 percent of the samples tested positive, the agreement called for once-a-year testing of players by name. In fact, between 5 and 7 percent of the 2003 samples tested positive, so the league began testing all players by name . . . [in 2004].

Anti-doping officials acknowledge they face an uphill battle in trying to stay ahead of pharmacological advances. Some banned substances—such as human growth hormone (HGH)—cannot be detected under current [2004] technology, and new drugs such as THG are designed to escape detection. Moreover, looming on the horizon is the possibility of so-called gene doping—manipulation of an athlete's genes—to improve performance. . . .

The Impact on Sports

Baseball fans were held spellbound in the late summer of 1998 as two of the game's leading sluggers—Mark McGwire and Sammy Sosa—chased one of the game's most daunting records: Roger Maris's mark of 61 home runs set nearly four decades earlier, in 1961. By the end of the season, the St. Louis Cardinals' first-baseman and Chicago Cubs' outfielder had both eclipsed the previous record, with Sosa at 66 and McGwire on top with a stunning 70 homers for the year.

As the home-run chase intensified, however, sports reporters noticed that the longtime power hitter [McGwire] had bottles of a dietary supplement called androstenedione—andro for short—in his locker. Questioned, McGwire openly acknowledged taking andro—a manufactured drug that the body converts into testosterone. Andro, which was legal for baseball players at the time, had already been banned in other sports—including football, collegiate athletics, and the Olympics.

Anti-doping officials . . . insist that performance-enhancing drugs hurt not only the image of competitive sport but the athletes as well.

The disclosure stirred a debate over the legitimacy of McGwire's feat. Some critics suggested that the eventual record needed to be marked with a doubt-casting asterisk. Most fans, however, appeared uninterested. And, tellingly, the sale of andro shot up thanks to the publicity.

Bowing to the controversy, MLB finally banned andros-tenedione on April 12, 2004.

Opposing Views

The episode illuminates the opposing views about performance-enhancing drugs in sports. Many fans may share the discomfort of anti-doping advocates who say that drugs tarnish the mythic purity of sports. "The public likes to have a clean game," says Don Catlin, director of the Olympic drug-testing laboratory at the University of California at Los Angeles. "They like it to be fair and square."

Anti-doping officials say some of the dangers are un-proven and many exaggerated.

But many fans also revel in the enhanced power, speed or endurance that steroids or other performance-enhancing drugs help make possible. "They love to see big, strong guys hit home runs," says Norman Fost, a professor of pediatrics at the University of Wisconsin Medical School and the most vocal academic opponent of anti-doping policies.

Fost has argued—all but alone in the United States—that anti-doping officials and advocates rely for their case on a fictitious image of pure athletic competition and exaggerated warnings of the health consequences of performance-enhancing drugs. He says they have been aided by compliant reporters who have conveyed those views to the public with little analysis and few doubts. "I can't think of a single subject that involves ethical and medical issues that's been so one-sided" in the media, Fost says.

Anti-doping officials, however, insist that performance-enhancing drugs hurt not only the image of competitive sport but the athletes as well. And steroid use by professional and Olympic athletes encourages young people to try them as well, they argue. "It's clearly something that's infiltrated its way down to grade school and up," says Gary I. Wadler, a professor at New York University Medical School and a member of WADA.

Medical authorities generally say that—for otherwise healthy people—steroids have few if any clinical benefits and produce serious side effects, even if not completely documented. Steroids increase cholesterol levels and, by implication, the risk of heart disease, they say. Oral steroids—though not the more common injected versions—also appear to be associated with liver cancer, they say. Anecdotal evidence suggests that steroids can produce hyper-aggressiveness in some users—so-called 'roid rage. And, for young people, steroids cause bones to stop growing, effectively stunting growth.

However, anti-doping officials say some of the dangers are unproven and many exaggerated. "There's no study that steroids cause heart attacks," says Larry Bowers, USADA's senior managing director for technical and information resources.

Yesalis, who has chided the media for "sensationalizing" the dangers from steroids, adds, "That doesn't mean there aren't potentially serious consequences."

Fost, however, says the dangers are greatly exaggerated. "There is a nearly uniform claim as to steroids that they're very dangerous, they can cause death, cancer, heart attacks," he says. "None of that is supported by any medical evidence, or at least it's widely exaggerated.". . .

But Fost agrees with anti-doping advocates on the risks steroids pose to young people. In fact, he favors continuing the ban for anyone under 18, pointing out that the most common use of steroids among young people is not by athletes but by bodybuilders. "It's middle- and high-school kids who want to look like Arnold Schwarzenegger," he says.

For adults, however, Fost says steroids and other performance-enhancing drugs should be legal, and deciding whether to use them should be left up to the individual athlete. "There's not a single athlete in any competitive sport who's just running on his or her natural ability," he says. "Why pick steroids to be concerned about?"

Steroids, Fost says, are conceptually indistinguishable from other manmade aids, such as fiberglass pole-vaulting poles or super-efficient swimsuits. As for the health consequences, Fost says many sports—from gymnastics to football—involve the risk of injury. "It's morally incoherent to prohibit adult athletes from risking harming themselves," he says.

Anti-doping advocates vigorously rebut Fost's arguments. "Why don't you legalize all these drugs?" asks Marc Safran, director of sports medicine at the University of California at San Francisco. "The winner would be the person who comes closer to risking their life."

Yesalis adds that performance-enhancing drugs take away a real but intangible part of the enduring appeal of sport. "You do not need drugs to have a sense of fulfillment, to feel that you've left it all on the field," Yesalis says. "[Drugs have] taken something that God has given us—love of game and sport—and perverted us."

Is Drug Testing Effective?

The controversy swirling around ... U.S. track stars stems not from failed drug tests but from a cloak-and-dagger story initiated by an anonymous tipster and a team of chemical sleuths. The newly discovered steroid THG was decoded by chemists at the Olympic drug-testing laboratory at UCLA [University of California, Los Angeles] from a sample delivered to USADA anonymously by someone who identified himself as a track and field coach.

Lab chief Catlin says it took three months of chemical testing to crack the code of the new steroid and develop a test to detect it—a chastening reminder of the difficulties of policing performance-enhancing drugs. "There are always new drugs moving in and the old ones moving out," he says.

Drug testing—which involves chemical analysis of athletes' urine or blood samples—has been the principal tool for anti-doping enforcement since its introduction in the 1950s. Drug testing snared its first Olympic medallist in 1972, when the teenage American swimmer Rick DeMont had to relinquish his gold medal after testing positive for the stimulant ephedrine, an ingredient in a prescription asthma medication he was taking. Then in 1984, Finnish runner Martti Vainio lost the silver medal he had won in the 10,000-meter race after testing positive for banned substances, and Canadian sprinter Ben Johnson was stripped of his gold medal in 1988 after testing positive for steroids.

The apparent simplicity and certainty of drug-test results, however, masks the complexity and uncertainty of the actual process. Testing is expensive—as much as $500 to $1,000 or more per test. Testing is susceptible to error, cover-up or even sabotage. And testing can be circumvented.

Athletes can sometimes escape detection at scheduled tests by halting the use of any banned substances beforehand. They also use more ingenious subterfuges. For instance, NFL players have been known to "borrow" urine specimens from someone else, hide the urine vial inside their athletic supporters and then—shielded by a partition—provide the examiner with the clean samples.

A Poor Performance Rating

Such problems lead many anti-doping advocates to dismiss drug testing as a failure. "The drug testing system has loopholes big enough that I could navigate an Abrams tank through it," Yesalis says. "It's been a colossal flop. I don't know what other enterprise that has such a poor performance rating would still be in business."

Meanwhile, drug tests have yet to be developed for some banned substances—notably, the synthetic human-growth hormone (HGH) and erynthropoietin (EPO), a hormone that stimulates production of oxygen-carrying red blood cells, which aid athletes in such endurance sports as cycling or marathons. And sports chemists are constantly developing new substances, such as THG, to evade detection.

"As long as there are people willing to cheat, there will be drugs that are undetectable," says Minnesota's Roberts. "This THG thing would never have come to light except that somebody blew the whistle."

Anti-doping critic Fost agrees. "The drugmakers and the athletes have kept ahead of the testers," he says. The inevitable futility of the effort is another reason to legalize performance-enhancing drugs, Fost suggests.

Some experts agree that a lifetime ban for a first doping violation is worth considering.

Moreover, legalizing the drugs would better protect athletes' health, he argues. "As long as they're banned, there will be people trying to avoid detection, and they'll have to do it underground," he says. "They'll be using drugs that won't be adequately tested or subject to [federal] oversight. The worst thing about the THG scandal is that anyone using it has no way of knowing what they're using."

Anti-doping officials acknowledge the difficulties but insist that testing is only one part of the overall effort to keep drugs out of sports. "What we're after is deterrence—not necessarily catching people and sanctioning them but deterring them from using drugs in the first place," USADA's Bowers says. "One of the tools we have for that is testing. We're better now than we were three years ago, and we're capable of seeing more things now than we were three years ago."

"You can't say that testing is going to stamp out drugs," says David Howman, WADA's director general. "You have to have effective education programs. We far prefer to be a preventive body than to be a detection body."

Are Penalties for Using Performance-Enhancing Drugs Stiff Enough?

Anti-doping advocates achieved an important breakthrough in 1999 when an international conference of sports organization and governments agreed to prescribe two-year suspensions for athletes' first doping violation and lifetime bans for a second offense. But U.S. Olympic sprinting champion Maurice Greene advocates even tougher penalties.

"There is no room in our sport for drug cheaters whatsoever," Greene said. "I don't think a year ban or a two-year ban is enough. I think it should be a life ban, if you get caught even once."

USA Track & Field voted last Dec. 7, 2003, to impose a lifetime ban for first-time steroid offenses. It has not yet been implemented, pending a determination that it does not violate the Amateur Sports Act.

Greene's outburst may not have been solely about anti-doping policies. He and Montgomery have a history of bad relations: It was Greene's record of 9.79 seconds in the 100-meter dash that Montgomery clipped in 2002. Greene—who has three of the four fastest times in the event—likes to remind listeners that Montgomery set his mark with a tailwind right at the limit allowed for official records.

Whatever Greene's motivation, some experts agree that a lifetime ban for a first doping violation is worth considering. "If you don't have very stiff penalties, you're not going to deter a lot of people," says the University of California's Safran. "A lifetime ban if you get caught would definitely get people to think twice about it."

Alternatives to a Lifetime Ban

But a lifetime ban might be too stringent to be enforceable, Bowers warns. "I'm not sure that we could get people to sanction athletes for life, particularly if that's their livelihood," he says. "If there's a repeat performance or lack of change in behavior after a first time, then I would support a lifetime ban."

In fact, the World Doping Code does allow reduced penalties for unintentional violations for banned substances found in generally available medicinal products. An athlete can also escape penalty by showing that he or she "bears no fault or negligence for the violation."

Legalization advocates see no reason for any penalties for using performance-enhancing drugs.

For his part, Catlin says, improved detection is more important than stiffened penalties. "There's enough punishment. A two-year penalty, that's strong enough," he says.

The debate over penalties is most squarely joined today [in 2004] regarding Major League Baseball. The penalties established this season as a result of the 2003 testing include, for a first offense, mandatory referral to treatment and counseling. For a second offense, the player would be suspended for 15 days; only after a fifth offense would a player be suspended for as long as a year. Fines also escalate—to as much as $100,000 for a fifth offense. . . .

Wadler calls the MLB penalties "woefully inadequate," noting that on a first offense, the only response is "'Go see a doctor.'"

For its part, the league is trying to reopen labor negotiations to provide for stiffer punishment. "The commissioner has been saying he'd like to see immediate discipline in the Major League policy," says Rob Manfred, MLB's executive vice president for labor relations.

But baseball association president Don Fehr insists mandatory treatment actually aids subsequent detection and prevention. "'Go see a doctor' began with a premise: If you test positive . . . there are going to be a lot more tests for you," Fehr says. "The likelihood of the conduct recurring diminishes very greatly."

On the other hand, legalization advocates see no reason for any penalties for using performance-enhancing drugs. "Athletes ought to be able to use them . . . under the supervision of a sports expert after careful clinical trials showing the benefits and risks," Fost says.

But Minnesota's Roberts says that if performance-enhancing drugs were legal, all athletes would feel pressured to use them. "If you're caught, you should be penalized and penalized to the point that it's not worth getting caught," Roberts says. "And if you're caught twice, you should be penalized for life. I would like for athletes to be able to compete without having to use them. A zero-tolerance policy would make that less likely."

2

Performance-Enhancing Drugs Are Harmful to Health

National Institute on Drug Abuse

The National Institute on Drug Abuse uses scientific research to improve prevention, treatment, and policy related to drug abuse.

The adverse side effects of performance-enhancing drugs range from temporary and permanent physical changes to stunted growth, heart complications, and serious infections. In some cases, the drugs can have a direct effect on increased irritability and aggression and can often lead to further drug use to counteract the negative side effects of anabolic steroids.

Anabolic steroid abuse has been associated with a wide range of adverse side effects ranging from some that are physically unattractive, such as acne and breast development in men, to others that are life threatening, such as heart attacks and liver cancer. Most are reversible if the abuser stops taking the drugs, but some are permanent, such as voice deepening in females.

Most data on the long-term effects of anabolic steroids in humans come from case reports rather than formal epidemiological studies. From the case reports, the incidence of life-threatening effects appears to be low, but serious adverse effects may be underrecognized or underreported, especially since they may occur many years later. Data from animal studies seem to support this possibility. One study found that exposing male mice for one-fifth of their lifespan to steroid

National Institute on Drug Abuse, "Anabolic Steroid Abuse," *Research Report Series*, September 2006, www.drugabuse.gov/PDF/RRSteroids.pdf.

doses comparable to those taken by human athletes caused a high frequency of early deaths.

Hormonal System

Steroid abuse disrupts the normal production of hormones in the body, causing both reversible and irreversible changes. Changes that can be reversed include reduced sperm production and shrinking of the testicles (testicular atrophy). Irreversible changes include male-pattern baldness and breast development (gynecomastia) in men. In one study of male bodybuilders, more than half had testicular atrophy and/or gynecomastia.

In the female body, anabolic steroids cause masculinization. Breast size and body fat decrease, the skin becomes coarse, the clitoris enlarges, and the voice deepens. Women may experience excessive growth of body hair but lose scalp hair. With continued administration of steroids, some of these effects become irreversible.

Musculoskeletal System

Rising levels of testosterone and other sex hormones normally trigger the growth spurt that occurs during puberty and adolescence and provide the signals to stop growth as well. When a child or adolescent takes anabolic steroids, the resulting artificially high sex hormone levels can prematurely signal the bones to stop growing.

Studies indicate that anabolic steroids, when used in high doses, increase irritability and aggression.

Cardiovascular System

Steroid abuse has been associated with cardiovascular diseases (CVD), including heart attacks and strokes, even in athletes younger than 30. Steroids contribute to the development of

CVD, partly by changing the levels of lipoproteins that carry cholesterol in the blood. Steroids, particularly oral steroids, increase the level of low-density lipoprotein (LDL) and decrease the level of high-density lipoprotein (HDL). High LDL and low HDL levels increase the risk of atherosclerosis, a condition in which fatty substances are deposited inside arteries and disrupt blood flow. If blood is prevented from reaching the heart, the result can be a heart attack. If blood is prevented from reaching the brain, the result can be a stroke.

Steroids also increase the risk that blood clots will form in blood vessels, potentially disrupting blood flow and damaging the heart muscle so that it does not pump blood effectively.

Liver

Steroid abuse has been associated with liver tumors and a rare condition called peliosis hepatis, in which blood-filled cysts form in the liver. Both the tumors and the cysts can rupture, causing internal bleeding.

Skin

Steroid abuse can cause acne, cysts, and oily hair and skin.

Infections

Many abusers who inject anabolic steroids may use nonsterile injection techniques or share contaminated needles with other abusers. In addition, some steroid preparations are manufactured illegally under nonsterile conditions. These factors put abusers at risk for acquiring life-threatening viral infections, such as HIV and hepatitis B and C. Abusers also can develop endocarditis, a bacterial infection that causes a potentially fatal inflammation of the inner lining of the heart. Bacterial infections also can cause pain and abscess formation at injection sites.

What Effects Do Anabolic Steroids Have on Behavior?

Case reports and small studies indicate that anabolic steroids, when used in high doses, increase irritability and aggression. Some steroid abusers report that they have committed aggressive acts, such as physical fighting or armed robbery, theft, vandalism, or burglary. Abusers who have committed aggressive acts or property crimes generally report that they engage in these behaviors more often when they take steroids than when they are drug free. A recent study suggests that the mood and behavioral effects seen during anabolic-androgenic steroid abuse may result from secondary hormonal changes.

Some users might turn to other drugs to alleviate some of the negative effects of anabolic steroids.

Scientists have attempted to test the association between anabolic steroids and aggression by administering high steroid doses or placebo for days or weeks to human volunteers and then asking the people to report on their behavioral symptoms. To date, four such studies have been conducted. In three, high steroid doses did produce greater feelings of irritability and aggression than did placebo, although the effects appear to be highly variable across individuals. In one study, the drugs did not have that effect. One possible explanation, according to the researchers, is that some but not all anabolic steroids increase irritability and aggression. Recent animal studies show an increase in aggression after steroid administration.

In a few controlled studies, aggression or adverse, overt behaviors resulting from the administration of anabolic steroid use have been reported by a minority of volunteers.

In summary, the extent to which steroid abuse contributes to violence and behavioral disorders is unknown. As with the health complications of steroid abuse, the prevalence of extreme cases of violence and behavioral disorders seems to be low, but it may be underreported or underrecognized.

Research also indicates that some users might turn to other drugs to alleviate some of the negative effects of anabolic steroids. For example, a study of 227 men admitted in 1999 to a private treatment center for addiction to heroin or other opioids found that 9.3 percent had abused anabolic steroids before trying any other illicit drug. Of these 9.3 percent, 86 percent first used opioids to counteract insomnia and irritability resulting from anabolic steroids.

Are Anabolic Steroids Addictive?

An undetermined percentage of steroid abusers may become addicted to the drugs, as evidenced by their continued abuse despite physical problems and negative effects on social relations. Also, steroid abusers typically spend large amounts of time and money obtaining the drugs, which is another indication that they may be addicted. Individuals who abuse steroids can experience withdrawal symptoms when they stop taking steroids, such as mood swings, fatigue, restlessness, loss of appetite, insomnia, reduced sex drive, and steroid cravings. The most dangerous of the withdrawal symptoms is depression, because it sometimes leads to suicide attempts. If left untreated, some depressive symptoms associated with anabolic steroid withdrawal have been known to persist for a year or more after the abuser stops taking the drugs.

3

The Demand for Performance-Enhanced Athletes Sends the Wrong Message

Judy Shepps Battle

Judy Shepps Battle is an addiction specialist, consultant, and freelance writer.

In pursuit of fame and fortune, some athletes choose to use dangerous performance-enhancing drugs. While it might be easy to blame the athletes themselves, the root problem is the public demand for spectacular sports entertainment—home runs, slam dunks, and broken records. Enhanced entertainment, however, blurs the line between true athletic prowess and enhanced performance, making it difficult to teach children the value of hard work. A better message would be to tell our children that not everyone can be a star athlete—that winning is not as important as how the game is played.

Given the American League award for Most Valuable Player in 2000, Jason Giambi signed with the New York Yankees for a reported seven-year, $120-million contract the following baseball season. Hitting 155 home runs and batting over 300 each season from 1999 to 2002, he earned the reputation of being a super-slugger and was a hero to kids of all ages.

Unfortunately his heroics on the ball diamond always will be clouded by the means through which he chose to achieve them.

Judy Shepps Battle, "Performance-Enhanced Sports: A Mirror of Society," *Join Together*, January 13, 2005. Reproduced by permission.

Giambi is the latest athlete to come clean with regard to use of variety of performance-enhancing substances—including self-injecting human growth hormone (hGH)—in pursuit of athletic fame and fortune. Faced with testifying before a grand jury, he reversed earlier denials that he cheated chemically for at least three seasons.

Giambi is certainly not the only athlete to use hGH. The hormone has been around for decades and is considered to be one of the most widely used banned substances in the sports world.

It is purported to increase muscle mass, allow faster recovery times after workouts, and—until recently [as of 2005]—has been virtually undetectable in standard drug-screening tests given to athletes. The 2004 Summer Olympics in Athens marked the first use of a blood test for hGH among competitors.

The Risks of hGH

What is less widely known is that abuse of hGH can cause high blood pressure, numbness in the fingers, fluid retention, and an increase in blood sugar. A user's liver, thyroid, and heart may be damaged, and acromegaly (a disease that causes bones in the hands, jaw, brow and feet to enlarge) may develop, researchers say.

[Children] quickly "get" the contradictory message— drugs are bad, but superhuman performance is good.

Teens whose bodies are still producing natural human growth hormone are at an even greater risk of harmful consequences from taking the substance. Instead of pumping up and growing stronger, taking hGH actually may cause a youth to shrink, as the excessive dose may cause joints to close.

However, the core of the problem is not hGH, the specific athletes who misuse it, or the legal ramifications involved—

indeed, it is highly unlikely any legal action will deter athletes from taking hGH. If the pressure to perform is great enough, the risk of getting caught will be ignored.

No, the core of the problem—the driving force behind the continued use of illegal performance-enhancing drugs—is the sports audience: you and me.

We, who have a seemingly insatiable desire to be entertained by these modern-day gladiators, are the real issue. We want thrills—slam-dunks, crushing tackles, perfect dives, Jason Giambi home runs—in exchange for our hefty admission fees.

Enhanced Entertainment

The reality is that in our society, enhanced entertainment is the norm, and it's in more than just the sports arena.

In a world where digital technology allows even the most mediocre musical performance to become outstanding or where "ordinary" people compete for million-dollar prizes by becoming island castaways, few are satisfied with watching athletes who are anything less than spectacular. This type of enhanced entertainment, however, can easily become confused with reality.

In the case of sports, the line between reality (genuine athletic prowess) and unreality (the enhanced performance of someone on hGH, for example) easily becomes blurred. Under such conditions, it becomes difficult to foster the power of determination and hard work that lies deep within each of us.

Most importantly, our children learn from our reaction to artificially enhanced entertainment. They quickly "get" the contradictory message—drugs are bad, but superhuman performance is good—and they are understandably confused when confronted with making personal decisions regarding use of performance enhancers.

We, as adults, must wean ourselves from supporting enhanced "reality" and show our kids that in real life, everyone is not a stellar athlete, that it really is more about how you play the game than whether you win.

Personally, I would love to see our new societal role models become those non-enhanced professional baseball players who struggle to hit 35 homers a year, or amateur runners who rejoice in completing a non-chemically assisted four-minute mile.

I would love to see our new society role models become those non-enhanced professional baseball players who struggle to hit 35 homers a year.

That's really what sports—and life—are all about.

4

The Athletic Benefits of Performance-Enhancing Drugs Are Exaggerated

Charley Reese

Charley Reese is a conservative journalist who has been working since 1955. While not a libertarian, Reese opposes big government and supports many free-market policies.

The actual athletic benefits of performance-enhancing drugs have been exaggerated. Indeed, use of performance-enhancing drugs will not make a star out of someone without talent. Babe Ruth, who did not train, consistently managed to hit home runs even after a night spent smoking and drinking because he had a natural gift. The real problem is that in the United States winning is considered everything. To prevent young people from choosing to use performance-enhancing drugs, Americans must instead teach children the importance of honesty and the joy of playing the game.

Yet another athlete faces hard times because of performance-enhancing drugs. This young man, Justin Gatlin, denies that he knowingly took the drug. He might be telling the truth. Young athletes put a lot of trust in their coaches, and this coach could have given him the drug and told him it was a vitamin.

Gatlin was tied for the world's record in the 100-meter dash. People in his hometown, Pensacola, Fla., speak highly of him and believe in his innocence. The drug test that was positive, however, might doom him. It seems to me that a mere test should not be sufficient to ruin a career. The officials ought to be required to prove that the athlete knowingly took the stuff.

Understanding Drugs and Users

Years ago, a friend of mine said that testing equipment had far outstripped human knowledge. He said tests could determine chemicals in as small an amount as a part per trillion. The problem is, nobody knows what effect, if any, a chemical in that small a quantity would have on a human being. He was talking about testing water supplies.

It could be, however, that not enough is known about testosterone. Does it really enhance performance? What other sources of the drug are there? What about the chemicals in energy drinks and energy bars? Is the test infallible? Are exact and proper procedures followed?

[Performance-enhancing drugs] might provide a thin margin to an already superbly conditioned athlete, but they won't make a star out of a slacker.

At any rate, a basic rule of criminal law is that one must prove not only that an act was committed, but that it was committed with criminal intent. If this young man just took what his trainers told him to take and didn't know that it contained testosterone, he should not be held accountable.

If the U.S. Anti-Doping Agency doesn't have a procedure to determine this, it should get one. Using testosterone is not a crime, but the penalty for an athlete is severe. If this young man is banned from track-and-field events for eight years, what's he going to do to make a living in the meantime? How good would he be at age 32, when he's reinstated?

Performance-enhancing drugs are a form of cheating. I'm generally against the practice. In fact, I get nostalgic about the good old days of amateur athletics, but the effects, I believe, have been exaggerated. They might provide a thin margin to an already superbly conditioned athlete, but they won't make a star out of a slacker.

One of the ironies of this current obsession with performance-enhancing drugs is that many of the old athletes didn't train at all. Babe Ruth often spent the night smoking, drinking, eating and carousing with women. He would show up at the ballpark hung over, eat 12 hot dogs and wash them down with six bottles of pop, then waddle out to the plate, his big belly emphasized by his spindly legs, and hit home runs. He had phenomenal eyesight, unusual depth perception, extremely good hand-eye coordination and lightning reflexes. Every one of those was a natural gift. You either have them or you don't.

An Obsession with Winning

The real solution to the drug problem starts with childhood. Americans have to get over this obsession that winning is everything. Children should be taught that there are things more important than winning, such as good behavior, honesty and the satisfaction of playing the game. Parents should teach children to be gracious in both victory and defeat. It is the obsession with winning that often drives young athletes to steroids and other drugs, and nine times out of 10 that obsession comes from demanding parents.

Winning is everything in a gunfight, but sports are just games to be played for enjoyment. It doesn't really matter who wins as long as both sides have a good time. The old Buddhist saying—Do your best, but don't worry about the outcome—applies to sports as well as to life in general.

When I covered high-school sports, I had an extremely low opinion of most coaches. They acted like drill instructors and were obsessed with winning. I wouldn't put up with their abusive barking for one second. One man, however, at a small Catholic high school made sure that every boy who wanted to play football made the team. He made sure everybody got a chance to play. The school had a poor record of wins, but he got my vote as outstanding coach of the year. He alone had the right priorities.

5

Looking for an Edge Is Part of Sports

Glenn Dickey

Glenn Dickey has covered San Francisco Bay Area sports since 1963. After forty-two years with the San Francisco Chronicle, *he is now a freelance writer. His columns appear in the San Francisco* Examiner *and on his Web site.*

In competitive sports, participants have always tried to gain an advantage—legally or illegally—over their adversaries. The U.S. pastime, baseball, is rife with examples: pitchers throw spitballs, hitters use corked bats, and groundskeepers slant baselines to their teams' advantage. The use of performance-enhancing drugs is simply one more strategy athletes use to gain an edge. Government money would be better spent on more important pursuits than the inevitable and unstoppable use of performance-enhancing drugs.

Could this BALCO steroids case get any more tawdry? [After a track coach sent the U.S. Anti-Doping Agency (USADA) a syringe of a new designer steroid—tetrahydrogestrinone or THG—in June 2003, federal and state authorities raided the offices of the Bay Area Laboratory Cooperative, BALCO, run by sports nutritionist Victor Conte, whose clients included baseball player Barry Bonds and some U.S. Olympic track stars. The raid led to a February 2004 indictment of Conte and others, alleging conspiracy to give athletes illegal steroids and prescription drugs. Conte, Greg

Glenn Dickey, "Cheating: Just Part of Game," *San Francisco Examiner,* February 16, 2007. Reproduced by permission.

Anderson, personal trainer for Bonds, and Patrick Arnold, an Illinois chemist who synthesized the THG, received short prison sentences and home detention for their illegal activities.] Now, the lawyer who once represented BALCO executives has admitted he defied a judge's order in leaking court documents to *San Francisco Chronicle* reporters, apparently in the hopes of forcing a mistrial motion.

Let's be honest about this: Despite the *Chronicle*'s repeated self-congratulations, this case has always been about self-interest, not journalistic integrity.

Abusing the Public's Right to Know

The reporters used the documents for a strong running story, which ultimately turned into a profitable book. The *Chronicle* used it in an attempt to win a Pulitzer Prize. The attempt failed, possibly because the Pulitzer committee felt a story based on court documents that were illegally leaked was not a great journalistic model.

There is a good reason that it's illegal to leak grand jury testimony: Jurors and witnesses alike need to know that their testimony and conversations will not be made public, so they can speak freely and honestly.

Athletes, coaches and managers are always going to be looking for that edge, whether it's in performance-enhancing drugs or alteration of playing equipment or fields.

Leaking testimony in a national security case or one that involves unconstitutional actions by the federal government can be justified. But leaking testimony about athletes taking performance-enhancing drugs? Please.

That's an unwarranted abuse of "the public's right to know."

Why are we even wasting time on this? What athletes are doing now is neither unprecedented or something that can be stopped.

Getting a Competitive Advantage

Though baseball generally and [home-run hitter] Barry Bonds [who continues to deny that he consciously took steroids] specifically are the targets of rage among American sports fans, there are many other examples of competitors in other sports trying to get a competitive advantage.

The NFL regularly catches steroid users. San Diego linebacker Shawn Merriman was suspended for four games [in the fall of 2006], though he still made the Pro Bowl.

Tour de France winner Floyd Landis has been accused of having high testosterone levels, a charge he is fighting, and other cyclists have been suspected, too. Drug use seems to be widespread among track and field competitors. NASCAR drivers have not been accused of drug use, but they regularly test the limits of restrictions on their cars; their criterion seems to be how far they can go without being caught.

Baseball itself has a long history of players and managers bending or breaking the rules to get an advantage.

Gaylord Perry was a young pitcher on his way out of baseball when he was taught to throw the spitball, which had been banned since 1920. With that pitch, he started a path to the baseball Hall of Fame—and even wrote a book about it.

On the other side, some famous hitters have been caught with corked bats, Sammy Sosa being the latest.

Groundskeepers have often slanted baselines to help their teams. Teams have stolen signs. Reportedly, the New York Giants had a man in the center-field bleachers with binoculars during the 1951 playoffs, so Bobby Thomson knew what was coming when he hit the famous home run against the Brooklyn Dodgers to send the Giants into the World Series.

We need to come to grips with the fact that athletes, coaches and managers are always going to be looking for that edge, whether it's in performance-enhancing drugs or alteration of playing equipment or fields.

If we just accept that, maybe we can move on, so the government isn't wasting time on trials about performance-enhancing drugs. Or in congressional hearings on the matter. There are more important subjects, even for sports fans.

6

Antidoping Policies Are Costly and Unethical

Bengt Kayser, Alexandre Mauron, and Andy Miah

Bengt Kayser is a professor of exercise physiology and Alexandre Mauron is a professor of bioethics at the Faculty of Medicine, University of Geneva, Switzerland. Andy Miah lectures on media, bioethics, and cyberculture at the University of Paisley in Scotland, and is author of Genetically Modified Athletes: Biomedical Ethics, Gene Doping and Sport.

Antidoping policies do not encourage fair play. In fact, many other factors, biological and environmental, also contribute to an athlete's performance. It is an ethical contradiction to object to those who enhance themselves with drugs while admiring those born with genetic enhancements. Claims that antidoping policies are necessary to protect athlete health are also contradictory, since most sports involve an increased risk of severe injury. In light of the fact that antidoping policies are based on groundless claims, the high cost of enforcing antidoping policies makes the strategy indefensible.

The rules of sport define a level playing field on which athletes compete. Antidoping policies exist, in theory, to encourage fair play. However, we believe they are unfounded, dangerous, and excessively costly.

The need for rules in sports cannot be dismissed. But the anchoring of today's antidoping regulations [as of 2005] in the notion of fair play is misguided, since other factors that affect performance—e.g., biological and environmental factors—are unchecked. Getting help from one's genes—by being blessed with a performance-enhancing genetic predisposition—is acceptable. Use of drugs is not. Yet both types of advantage are undeserved. Prevailing sports ethics is unconcerned with this contradiction.

Another ethical foundation for antidoping concerns the athlete's health. Antidoping control is judged necessary to prevent damage from doping. However, sport is dangerous even if no drugs are taken—playing soccer comes with high risks for knee and ankle problems, for instance, and boxing can lead to brain damage. To comprehensively assess any increase in risk afforded by the use of drugs or technology, every performance-enhancing method needs to be studied. Such work cannot be done while use of performance-enhancing drugs is illegal. We believe that rather than drive doping underground, use of drugs should be permitted under medical supervision.

> As the costs of antidoping control rises year on year, ethical objections are raised that are . . . weightier than the ethical arguments advanced for antidoping.

The Advantage of Legalisation

Legalisation of the use of drugs in sport might even have some advantages. The boundary between the therapeutic and ergogenic—i.e., performance enhancing—use of drugs is blurred at present and poses difficult questions for the controlling bodies of antidoping practice and for sports doctors. The antidoping rules often lead to complicated and costly administrative and medical follow-up to ascertain whether drugs taken by athletes are legitimate therapeutic agents or illicit.

If doping was allowed, would there be an increase in the rate of death and chronic illness among athletes? Would athletes have a shorter lifespan than the general population? Would there be more examples like the widespread use of performance-enhancing drugs in the former East German Republic? We do not think so. Only a small proportion of the population engages in elite sports. Furthermore, legalisation of doping, we believe, would encourage more sensible, informed use of drugs in amateur sport, leading to an overall decline in the rate of health problems associated with doping. Finally, by allowing medically supervised doping, the drugs used could be assessed for a clearer view of what is dangerous and what is not.

The role of the doctor is to preserve the patient's best interests with respect to present and future health. A sports doctor has to fulfil this role while maintaining the athlete's performance at as high a level as possible. As such, as long as the first condition is met, any intervention proven safe, pharmacological or otherwise, should be justified, irrespective of whether or not it is ergogenic. A doctor who tries to enhance the performance of the athlete should not be punished for the use of pharmacological aids, but should be held accountable for any ill effects. Rather than speculate on antidoping test procedures, resources should be invested into protecting the integrity of doctors who make such judgments.

Acknowledging the importance of rules in sports, which might include the prohibition of doping, is, in itself, not problematic. However, a problem arises when the application of these rules is beset with diminishing returns: escalating costs and questionable effectiveness. The ethical foundation of prohibiting the use of ergogenic substances in sports is weak. As the cost of antidoping control rises year on year, ethical objections are raised that are, in our view, weightier than the ethical arguments advanced for antidoping. In the competition between increasingly sophisticated doping—e.g., gene transfer—and antidoping technology, there will never be a clear winner. Consequently, such a futile but expensive strategy is difficult to defend.

7

Prohibitions Against Performance-Enhancing Drugs Should Be Repealed

Jacob Sullum

Jacob Sullum, senior editor of Reason, *a monthly libertarian magazine, is a syndicated newspaper columnist who writes about controversial issues, including drug policy. Sullum is author of* For Your Own Good: The Anti-Smoking Crusade and the Tyranny of Public Health.

Athletic organizations should repeal prohibitions against performance-enhancing drugs. Not only are the benefits of drugs such as testosterone unproven, but the distinction between natural and artificial enhancements is flawed. In addition to taking advantage of natural enhancements such as the improved endurance that accompanies living in high altitudes, athletes use all sorts of unnatural technology to improve their performance. Allowing all forms of enhancement, natural and artificial, would truly level the playing field.

After winning the Tour de France [in 2006], Floyd Landis was hailed as an American hero who epitomized all that is good and glorious about cycling. A few days later, when it was announced that a urine test he took during the tour had revealed a suspiciously high ratio of testosterone to epitestosterone, he was condemned as a cheater who had disgraced the sport, perhaps ruining it forever.

Testosterone is powerful stuff, causing outbursts of anger and anxiety in people who have not even taken it. The antidote for those reactions is not a renewed commitment to drug-free sports but the acceptance of steroids as one of many tools athletes use to enhance their performance.

First let me state the obvious: Cheating is wrong. If you agree to follow certain rules, no matter how arbitrary or silly they may be, you should follow them.

Yet if you believe no one else follows them—an impression reinforced by the very sportswriters who bemoan the ubiquity of performance-enhancing drugs—the temptation not to be the only chump who does is strong. Furthermore, widespread violation of the rules, despite testing and severe sanctions, casts doubt on their wisdom.

The rules' supporters seem to think steroid use and other banned methods fundamentally change an athletic contest. "We have signed a television contract for a sports event and not for a display of the performance of pharmaceuticals," said the editor in chief of the German TV network ZDF, threatening to drop coverage of the Tour de France in response to the Landis scandal.

Exaggerating Performance-Enhancing Drugs' Power

That over-the-top reaction, typical of the angry, hurt tone that pervades commentary about once-admired athletes implicated in doping, grossly exaggerates the power of performance-enhancing drugs. Testosterone, for example, helps build muscle and hasten recovery during training, but as an expert on the hormone told the *New York Times*, "no one has been able to show clearly that testosterone improves endurance" during a competition.

Landis may have believed a short-term testosterone boost would help him win one of the world's most grueling athletic contests. But it probably had little or no effect on his performance in Stage 17, when he climbed from 11th to third place, gritting his teeth through the pain caused by a degenerative hip condition.

Instead of arbitrarily prohibiting certain [performance-enhancing] techniques, why not level the playing field by repealing the prohibitions?

To judge from some of the hand wringing over Landis' test results, however, any cyclist could have done just as well, given the right dose of testosterone. *New York Times* sports columnist Bill Rhoden, who called Landis' performance "an exhilarating exhibition of strength, speed, ingenuity and heart," simultaneously worried that "everything we think we see" in athletics "is little more than a sports mirage."

Suppose Landis was telling the truth when he claimed he had naturally high testosterone levels, and suppose this characteristic gave him a competitive edge. Would that render his amazing accomplishment a "mirage"? Obviously not, unless an athlete's innate talent also gives him an unfair advantage and makes him a fake.

To see how untenable the natural/artificial distinction is, consider altitude tents and rooms, which simulate the low-oxygen environment of high elevations in an attempt to improve endurance by spurring the production of red blood cells. The World Anti-Doping Association is considering a ban on this widely used technique, which its ethics committee deems contrary to "the spirit of sport."

If performance-enhancing drugs violate "the spirit of sport," it's hard to see why performance-enhancing rooms don't. If anything, they're even less natural than steroids. Yet banning high-altitude simulations arguably would make contests *less* fair, giving an advantage to athletes who happen to live at high elevations or who can afford to move there.

Athletes use all sorts of technology to improve their fitness and performance, ranging from multivitamins to weight machines, and they are properly judged by how well they use them. Instead of arbitrarily prohibiting certain techniques, why not level the playing field by repealing the prohibitions?

8

Athletic Governing Bodies Should Administer Drug Testing Programs

Matthew J. Mitten

Matthew J. Mitten is a law professor and director of the National Sports Law Institute, at Marquette University Law School, in Milwaukee, Wisconsin. Mitten chairs the National Collegiate Athletics Association's Competitive Safeguards and Medical Aspects of Sports Committee, which oversees the NCAA's drug education and testing program for student athletes.

While performance-enhancing drugs are federally controlled substances and Congress does have jurisdiction to establish a drug-testing program for professional athletes, the athletic governing bodies themselves are in a better position to establish and implement drug-testing programs for professional athletes. Federal involvement in pro sports is inappropriate and unnecessary. The governing bodies of pro sports already have testing procedures in place that have in fact reduced the use of steroids. Since many performance-enhancing drugs are illegal, the government should focus on preventing access to these drugs and prosecuting those who distribute them.

Some athletes at all levels of sports competition are willing to use banned performance-enhancing drugs, even though doing so violates the rules of the game and exposes them to sanctions, could adversely affect their health, and may violate federal or state laws. Several former Major League Baseball and National Football League players such as Jose Canseco, Ken Caminiti (deceased), Bill Romanowski, and Steve Courson have admitted using anabolic steroids to enhance their onfield performances. Prominent Olympic athletes (e.g., Ben Johnson and Jerome Young) have tested positive for steroid use, and other Olympians are suspected or accused of using steroids. Approximately one percent of the 11,000 National Collegiate Athletic Association student-athletes who randomly are tested each year [as of 2005] come up positive for usage of banned performance-enhancing substances. According to a 2003 Centers for Disease Control and Prevention survey of ninth to 12th graders, steroid use by high school students has more than doubled from 1991 to 2003—to more than six percent.

Anabolic steroids, when combined with vigorous physical training, do enhance athletic performance by making users bigger, stronger, and faster—while also speeding up their recovery time after strenuous exercise. If steroids effectively enhance performance, what is wrong with allowing athletes to take advantage of modern medicine and pharmacology? After all, athletes frequently are given painkillers and are fitted with artificial devices designed to enable continued participation in a sport despite an injury, and these generally are considered to be acceptable practices. Although there is concern about potential health risks, libertarians point to the current lack of compelling medical evidence that steroid usage by adult athletes causes serious health risks beyond those already inherent in competitive sports. Some commentators, including physicians, advocate allowing athletes to use steroids with medical supervision after full disclosure regarding their known health risks rather than banning and imposing sanctions for their usage.

Is there really an appropriate line that can be drawn between legitimate athletic performance enhancement through artificial means and unethical doping to achieve an unfair competitive advantage? For example, athletes' usage of artificially created low-oxygen living environments in low-altitude training areas currently is permitted, whereas their use of erythropoietin (EPO) to achieve similar effects is prohibited by sports governing bodies. Moreover, who is the appropriate entity to draw this line?

The Role of Governing Bodies

Perhaps it is easier to answer both questions by considering the second question first. Sports governing bodies have a legitimate interest in establishing uniform rules necessary to maintain the sport's integrity and image, ensure competitive balance, and protect athletes' health and safety. Although achieving maximum individual performance and winning is the objective of athletic competition, the essence of sports is that all participants play by the same rules. Antidoping regulations are an integral part of the "rules of the game," similar to those regulating playing equipment, scoring competition results, and penalizing infractions. Even if a sport's rules of play are arbitrary (and they often are), the sport's governing body has the inherent authority to promulgate clearly defined boundaries to ensure fair play and enforce them in a uniform, nondiscriminatory manner.

Moreover, anabolic steroids are a federally controlled substance. Medical experts have identified several potential negative side effects of using them. Clinical experiments involving athletes' use of steroids solely to improve onfield performance would raise serious ethical issues. For example, East German athletes who were given steroids under medical supervision, which enabled them to win Olympic medals during the Cold War era, now are suffering serious adverse health effects.

Courts and arbitration panels have upheld the legal authority of sports governing bodies (and educational institutions) to use random urinalysis drug testing of high school, college, and Olympic athletes. These tribunals generally conclude that protecting the integrity of athletic competition and sports participants' health and safety outweigh athletes' legitimate privacy interests. An athlete who uses these banned substances is a "cheater" whose unethical conduct may be punished.

Athletes who use prohibited substances directly expose themselves to potential adverse health consequences and indirectly subject others to similar risks. By nature, many athletes are risk-takers who will adopt their counterparts' successful training methods—even dangerous ones—if doing so enhances their performance. Thus, other athletes' actual or perceived usage of steroids creates a strong incentive to "level the playing field," which may cause an individual who would not otherwise ingest or inject steroids to do so.

The Testing Protocols

Pharmacological performance-enhancing substances are banned because of their adverse effects on both athletes' health and competitive integrity. For example, the World Anti-Doping Agency (WADA) Code only prohibits usage of a substance that satisfies at least two of the following criteria: it enhances or has the potential to enhance sports performance; it creates an actual or potential health risk; or it violates the spirit of sport. No single criteria is a sufficient reason for prohibiting usage. For example, the first criteria includes the use of creatine and artificial low-oxygen living environments, which are permitted because neither of the other criteria presently are deemed to be satisfied. Conversely, the use of anabolic steroids is prohibited because at least two, and arguably all three, of these criteria have been met.

The WADA Code governs Olympic sports competition. It generally provides for strict liability and mandatory minimum suspensions for athletes' usage of banned substances. Pursuant to a contract with the United States Olympic Committe

[USOC] the United States Anti-Doping Agency (USADA), an independent entity, administers and oversees the drug-testing program for American Olympic athletes. An individual has the right to appeal USADA's finding of a doping violation to an arbitral tribunal and to seek a reduced sanction because of mitigating circumstances.

The NCAA [National Collegiate Athletic Association] has a random drug-testing protocol applicable to all student-athletes participating in its member institutions' intercollegiate athletics program. It provides for strict liability and a one-year suspension from participation in all NCAA sports (along with a loss of one year of eligibility) for testing positive for a banned substance, with the right to an administrative appeal before members of the NCAA's Competitive Safeguards and Medical Aspects of Sports' drug education and testing subcommittee. Effective Aug. 1, 2005, the NCAA's drug-testing protocol was modified to make it more consistent with the WADA Code by withholding an athlete from NCAA competition who is under a doping suspension by a national or international sports governing body that has adopted the WADA Code, and by allowing consideration of a reduced penalty for a positive test in extenuating circumstances.

Because of the large number of students participating in interscholastic athletics and the high cost of testing ($50–100 per test), no state high school athletics governing body at present requires testing for performance-enhancing drugs. For the same reasons, very few school districts test for anabolic steroids. The California Interscholastic Federation, which regulates the state's high school athletics, recently adopted a policy to curb steroid use. It requires a student and his or her parents to agree in writing that the athlete will not use steroids without a physician's prescription and that coaches complete a certification program having a significant component regarding steroids and performance-enhancing dietary supplements. It also prohibits school-related personnel and groups from selling, distributing, or advocating the use of muscle-building dietary supplements.

The Penalties for Pros

Professional team sport athletes such as Major League Baseball, National Basketball Association, National Football League, and National Hockey League players generally have chosen to unionize, and drug-testing programs are a mandatory subject of collective bargaining. Thus, unlike the USOC, NCAA, and the governing bodies for nonunionized professional sports, MLB and the NBA, NFL, and NHL cannot unilaterally impose drug-testing programs on their players. The NFL and NBA have had collectively bargained mandatory drug-testing programs for several years.

As part of the Bay Area Laboratory Co-Operative (BALCO) grand jury investigation into the illegal sale and distribution of THC, several prominent baseball players were called to testify in December 2003, regarding whether they used anabolic steroids to enhance their athletic performance. In the wake of this scandal, Pres. Bush, in his 2004 State of the Union Address, urged professional sports leagues to adopt voluntarily more stringent drug policies that effectively will eliminate steroid use and set a better example for America's youth. In January 2005, Major League Baseball and its players union established their first testing program for performance-enhancing drugs.

Athletic governing bodies are in the best position to establish appropriate drug-testing programs in order to regulate the permissible bounds of competition and to protect athletes' health and safety.

Current penalties for a first drug testing violation are unpaid suspensions of 10 days for MLB players, four games for NFL players, and 10 games for NBA players. Meanwhile, the

NHL's new policy, negotiated through collective bargaining after last year's lockout (non)season, has yet to be made public.

Federal Proposals

To protect public health and safety, the federal government recently [as of 2005] has taken steps to restrict access to performance-enhancing drugs and prevent their usage by athletes (particularly youthful ones). Anabolic steroids have been federally regulated since 1990. However, many athletes used steroid precursors, which were sold as legal over-the-counter dietary supplements under the Dietary Supplement Health and Education Act of 1994. Except for dehydroepiandrosterone (DHEA), steroid precursors now are regulated by the Anabolic Steroid Control Act of 2004, which became effective Jan. 20, 2005. As reflected by the BALCO grand jury proceeding, the federal government also is actively prosecuting those who illegally provide performance-enhancing drugs to athletes.

In addition to these measures, there have been several 2005 congressional committee hearings regarding professional athletes' use of steroids and proposed federal laws to reduce their demand for these substances. These bills would establish a uniform random drug testing policy for professional athletes, with substantial fines imposed on sports organizations for failing to implement and comply with this policy.

The Clean Sports Act of 2005—which by no means is guaranteed to become law—is intended "to protect the integrity of professional sports and the health and safety of athletes generally," with the objectives of eliminating performance-enhancing substances. This proposed legislation would apply only to the NFL, NBA, NHL, MLB, Major League Soccer, Arena Football, and the United States Boxing Commission, which must develop drug-testing policies and procedures as stringent as those of USADA. However, the proposed bill provides the sense of Congress that all professional sports leagues should comply with these standards. Each athlete would be tested five times annually. There would be a mandatory two-year suspension for a first offense and a lifetime ban for a second offense, with the possibility of a reduced penalty for unknown or unsuspected usage of a banned substance. [The bill remained in committee as of May 2007.]

The sport's governing body should have the exclusive authority to establish sanctions that effectively reduce athletes' incentives to engage in doping.

The Director of the Office of National Drug Control Policy would be empowered to include other professional sports leagues or NCAA colleges and athletes within the Act's coverage based on a determination that doing so would prevent the use of performance-enhancing substances by high school, college, or professional athletes. Noncompliance with the Act's substantive provisions would constitute unfair or deceptive acts or practices in violation of the Federal Trade Commission Act with a potential civil penalty of $1,000,000 per violation.

The Secretary of Commerce would be directed to promulgate regulations requiring testing for steroids and other performance-enhancing substances and may fine a professional sports league $5,000,000 for failing to adopt testing policies and procedures consistent with the regulations.

With some variations, similar bills titled the Professional Sports Integrity and Accountability Act and the Professional Sports Integrity Act of 2005 have been introduced in the Senate and House, respectively. [Both bills remained in committee as of May 2007.] Do not be surprised if more legislative proposals are on the way.

Constitutional Challenges

Congress clearly has jurisdiction to establish a drug-testing program for professional leagues based on its authority to regulate interstate commerce, and there are other potential bases for enacting such legislation. Nevertheless, professional athletes and their unions may assert that federally mandated drug testing violates their rights under the Constitution. Targeted drug testing of professional athletes, but not other private employees, is inconsistent treatment. However, the federal equal protection clause requires only a rational basis to justify treating professional athletes differently, which is satisfied by their prominence in American society and imitation by youngsters.

> *Rather than imposing an external drug-testing program on sports organizations, the federal government should focus on preventing access to performance-enhancing drugs that pose health risks.*

A more interesting issue is whether mandatory drug testing of adult professional athletes without an individualized suspicion of illegal drug usage constitutes an unreasonable "search" in violation of the Fourth Amendment. In recent years, the Supreme Court has upheld mandatory random drug testing of high school athletes for recreational drugs by public educational institutions to protect their health and safety. Other courts have rejected college athletes' legal challenges to mandatory random drug testing for performance-enhancing and recreational drugs as a condition of participation in intercollegiate athletics. This judicial precedent, which holds that random drug testing is an appropriate means of maintaining the integrity of amateur athletic competition and protecting athletes' health, also may be applied to professional sports.

Although Congress may have valid regulatory authority, this proposed federal legislation inappropriately would interfere with the internal governance of professional sports, which historically have not been subject to direct government regulation. Athletic governing bodies are in the best position to establish appropriate drug-testing programs in order to regulate the permissible bounds of competition and to protect athletes' health and safety. The primary harm that results from athletes' usage of banned performance-enhancing substances is to the sport's integrity. Thus, the sport's governing body should have the exclusive authority to establish sanctions that effectively reduce athletes' incentives to engage in doping. Market considerations, combined with political pressure, should provide a strong economic incentive for a professional sports league and its players union to establish an effective drug-testing program. For example, MLB recently adopted its first testing program for performance-enhancing substances in response to these factors. Its program appears to be reducing steroid usage by its players, although Baseball Commissioner Bud Selig has called for more severe penalties than befell the Baltimore Orioles' Rafael Palmiero, a first-time offender who tested positive for steroids after testifiying under oath at a congressional hearing in March [2005] that he does not used banned or illegal substances.

Rather than imposing an external drug-testing program on sports organizations, the federal government should focus on preventing access to performance-enhancing drugs that pose health risks and prosecuting persons who distribute these substances illegally. The government potentially could fine and imprison athletes for violating controlled substances laws by knowingly using illegal performance-enhancing substances, which would penalize them for the indirect harm caused to American youths who view professional athletes as role models and emulate their conduct. (However, the International Olympic Committee is opposed to using criminal law to punish sports doping.) Both the federal government and sports governing bodies have important roles to play in eradicating the use of banned performance-enhancing substances by athletes. However, their respective roles should be complementary rather than overlapping.

9

Federal Involvement in Policing Athletes Entitles Athletes to Due Process

Dionne L. Koller

Dionne L. Koller is assistant professor of law at the University of Baltimore School of Law, in Maryland.

Olympic athletes accused of using performance-enhancing drugs based on evidence obtained in federal investigations are entitled to due process protections. The U.S. Anti-Doping Agency (USADA) claims that it need not provide constitutional protections to athletes under its purview because it is a private agency. However, the USADA is catching athletes who use performance-enhancing drugs by obtaining information from federal investigations. If agencies such as the USADA are going to use government power, they must offer these athletes the constitutional protections that accompany such exercises of power.

For those who are concerned with government encroachment on the civil rights of its citizens, a recent news report about the government's collaboration with the U.S. Anti-Doping Agency (USADA) should give pause.

The article in the *Washington Post* noted the benefits of the "unique" partnership between the anti-doping agency and the government whereby the USADA was able to sanction amateur athletes and ban them from competition with the indispensable aid of Uncle Sam. It featured quotes from anti-

doping officials explaining that with the tools of government—such as wiretaps and documents seized as part of
federal investigations—the agency can achieve results it could
not on its own.

Questioning the Power of the USADA

As Don Catlin, director of UCLA's [University of California,
Los Angeles'] Olympic Analytical Laboratory, which assists the
USADA, said of the government's involvement in anti-doping
efforts: "It has clearly caused a revolution. Sports authorities
have no power to do anything and government has the power
to do all. That's what it takes."

If that is in fact what it takes, and if we want the government going after sports cheats (and helping to get them out of
competition), there is one little catch. The alleged cheats are
entitled to constitutional due process protections. That is because the Constitution is supposed to apply to exercises of
government—as opposed to private—power. It's a bedrock
principle of constitutional law.

The USADA maintains that it is "private" and so does not
have to give constitutional protections to the athletes it sanctions and bans from competition. It claims this despite the
fact that it was created by and through the efforts of the federal government, receives most of its funding through the federal government, and works closely with the federal government to develop its cases against accused athletes and
ultimately ban them from competition.

*Olympic athletes . . . do not waive their due process rights
by virtue of the fact that they can run 100 meters in less
than 10 seconds.*

The anti-doping agency was established in 2000 through
the efforts of federal drug czar Barry R. McCaffrey and the
Office of National Drug Control Policy. Mr. McCaffrey and

members of Congress such as Republican senators John McCain of Arizona and Ted Stevens of Alaska had had enough of the reports of cheating by U.S. Olympic athletes. A worldwide movement was afoot to establish uniform standards for testing and sanctions for doping offenses.

The United States took a lead role in these efforts, and as part of that it directed the U.S. Olympic Committee to cease its ineffective drug testing program and create the anti-doping agency. The Olympic committee complied, and the USADA began operations designated by Congress as the United States' "official" anti-doping agency. Senators McCain and Stevens as well as other members of Congress had dreams of giving the agency jurisdiction over testing for professional sports as well, but the pro leagues thus far have resisted.

In 2004, shortly before the Athens Olympics, the BALCO [Bay Area Laboratories Cooperative] scandal broke. In addition to uncovering an illegal performance-enhancing drug distribution operation, federal agents also learned that several elite track and field athletes, many of whom were Olympic hopefuls, were allegedly customers. The problem for the USADA was that the drug sold by BALCO was a specially engineered, undetectable steroid, so none of the athletes who allegedly used the drug failed a drug test.

To keep "cheaters" from going to the Olympic Games, Mr. McCain and the Senate Commerce Committee took the extraordinary step of subpoenaing the documents from the ongoing federal investigation and turning them over to the USADA so that it could ban the accused athletes from competition.

This action was considered unprecedented because prosecutors do not share secret grand jury documents. But for the good of the country and its Olympic image, federal prosecutors did just that. And judging by the reports on the recent crackdown in Florida on illegal Internet sales of steroids and other performance-enhancing substances, they are continuing to do it, aiding the USADA in its work to defeat dopers by giving it evidence on athletes that the agency could not get as a regular "private" entity.

What is wrong with catching athletes who cheat? Nothing. But if you are a fan of constitutional limits on government power, you should be nervous. The USADA is accomplishing its mission through the use of government power. And through winks and nods, it asserts its "private" status while enjoying the fruits of that government power, without those pesky constitutional side effects.

Olympic athletes may be very different from you and me, but they are citizens, and they do not waive their due process rights by virtue of the fact that they can run 100 meters in less than 10 seconds.

10

Testing Inhibits the Development of Performance-Enhancing Drugs

Ken Mannie

Ken Mannie is head strength and conditioning coach at Michigan State University.

Designer steroids are new drugs that have been designed to mimic the muscle-building effect of testosterone and to evade detection in tests. As long as athletes are willing to risk their health to improve their performance, unscrupulous biochemists will design new performance-enhancing drugs with the goal of evading detection. To attack this problem, the sports community must work aggressively to stay abreast of new performance-enhancing drugs, implement rigorous testing procedures at all levels of sport, and institute strict penalties for those who use these drugs.

The word is out, the media are pointing fingers, subpoenas have been issued, and many athletes are running for cover. "Designer" steroids are in the news and circulating in the bloodstreams of some very successful, unethical, and unintelligent athletes—and the situation appears to be getting uglier by the minute.

Exactly what is a designer steroid? Simply put, it is an anabolic drug that has been structurally manipulated to mimic the muscle-building effects of testosterone while sidestepping a positive test result. The drug designers are very well-versed

Ken Mannie, "Designer Steroids: Ugly and Dangerous," *Join Together*, March 10, 2004. Reproduced by permission.

on the mechanisms of the current testing technology, and have the bioengineering expertise necessary to fool the system.

Those of us who hold sacred the integrity of athletics at all levels must understand that we are not dealing with some college kids delving in bathtub chemistry. Individuals with serious scientific acumen are on a mission to produce the perfect performance-enhancing drugs—ones that build muscle and are invisible.

The Age of Stealth Steroids

ESPN recently reported that more than 40 track athletes have been subpoenaed to testify before a federal grand jury investigating a prominent sports "nutritionist" on what is being called an international doping conspiracy. Several track and field performers have tested positive for Tetrahydrogestrinone, or THG, which is the most talked-about designer steroid.

Even more frightening than this discovery is that many experts say that THG may be only one of a bevy of other chemicals that unscrupulous biochemists have feverishly produced to fly under the testing radar. Now that THG is detectable, the questions remain: How long have athletes been using this stuff and what else is out there that we still can't detect? Could there be a multitude of these undetectable compounds in the illegal, performance-enhancing drug pipeline?

Terry Madden, director of the U.S. Anti-Doping Agency, calls the THG case "intentional doping of the worst kind." And while track and field is being indicted as a major offender of THG abuse, other sports—including the NFL, NHL, and Major League Baseball—are being scrutinized for having potential participants in this dangerous game of hormonal roulette. As a matter of fact, the International Olympic Committee and the NFL are considering retroactive testing of urine samples to examine the extent of THG abuse. This could result in medals being stripped and suspensions being imposed.

For some inexplicable reason, however, MLB and the NHL are still dragging their prehistoric knuckles on implementing year-round, random, unannounced steroid testing. This "hear no evil, see no evil, speak no evil" mentality continues to erode the credibility of these sports and victimizes the clean players through guilt by association. The ugly possibilities presented by these recent revelations make corked bats and spitballs seem relatively insignificant.

The Scope of the Problem

The scourge of illicit anabolic-steroid abuse in athletics is nothing new; artificial steroids were formulated back in the 1930s for treating a host of muscle-wasting diseases and sexual dysfunctions. However, the reported dosages used for performance-enhancement and/or increased muscular size are 10–100 times the medical indications.

Unprincipled doctors, coaches, and athletes have channeled the drugs into sports. Their motive is simple: bigger, stronger muscles can equate [to] more strength and speed, and steroids offer a potential shortcut to that end. That assumption can be debated to a degree, but most experts seem to agree that steroids—when combined with aggressive training protocols—can achieve intended goals at a faster rate and to a higher level in most cases.

Many people who abuse steroids are not athletes. They are everyday Joes and Janes who have self-esteem issues about their bodies or are simply looking for a cosmetic quick fix.

Among adolescents, a survey conducted by the National Institute on Drug Abuse (NIDA) found a significant increase in steroid use in 8th- to 12th-graders from 1991–1999. Among [high-school] seniors, there is also a noted decrease in the perceived harmful effects of the drugs. Whatever we're doing in our schools from an educational standpoint doesn't appear to be taking hold.

The bottom line: More kids are using steroids, and, for some unknown reasons, they erroneously believe that the health risks have mysteriously diminished.

[The sports community must] stay ahead of the testing tit-for-tat game so that our technology is up to snuff with the clandestine labs that are hard at work hood-winking the system.

Kids are taking steroids in a variety of ways, including orally, through intramuscular injection, and even in gels or creams that are rubbed on the skin. Contrary to the reports in underground publications, there is no scientifically substantiated "safe" way to put these drugs into your body. Some users believe that you can avoid negative side-effects by "cycling" or "pyramiding" the doses from low to high for 6 to 12 weeks, then backing-off for a few weeks before resuming the process. The efficacy of these techniques is strictly anecdotal, with no sound science to support any one method for all individuals.

Over-The-Counter Pills

The Anabolic Steroid Control Act of 1990 banned the distribution of all known steroids. However, Congress could not foresee the new wave of over-the-counter (OTC) drugs known as "pro-steroids" and "precursor steroids." Two compounds in the pro-steroid classification are 1-testosterone and 4-hydroxy-testosterone, which escaped mention in the legislation because they were virtually unknown. The drug manufacturers claim that these are "natural" substances, and market them as dietary supplements that increase strength and build muscle.

These anabolic compounds have surfaced on nutrition-store shelves in alarming numbers. They have all the markings of full-blown anabolic steroids, so did these chemicals slip through the legal barriers and proliferate as OTC dietary supplements? The steroid precursors convert to illegal drugs only after they have been ingested. And some of the pro-steroids—which are much more potent than the precursors because they don't require conversion in the body—are either difficult to detect, or are undetectable by current testing procedures.

The exposure of the designer-steroid conspiracy should serve as a wake-up call to all coaches, administrators, parents, [school] governing bodies . . . and state and federal lawmakers.

The deleterious effects of using these so-called supplements, however, are considered by many experts to be just as serious as with any other class of anabolic steroids. Athletes, coaches, and administrators must be cognizant of these OTC products and thoroughly examine the labels on any purchased supplements for potentially dangerous steroidal compounds. Someone who is qualified to identify these chemicals on the list of ingredients should be called on before any supplement distribution takes place.

Proactive Solutions

The sports community must come to the realization that fortune and fame—rather than ethics and fair play—are the motivational fuel for many athletes. And there will always be plenty of chemists willing to satisfy those needs through any means necessary, as their motivation is strictly monetary.

Those of us who have the power and resources to curb this problem must take off the gloves and attack it aggressively on several fronts:

- Stay ahead of the testing tit-for-tat game so that our technology is up to snuff with the clandestine labs that are hard at work hoodwinking the system.

- Incorporate the best testing procedures at the collegiate, professional, and international levels on a year-round, random, and unannounced basis.

- Institute strict penalties for athletes who test positive for anabolic drugs.

- Encourage the Food and Drug Administration (FDA) to take more of a proactive role in regulating the OTC supplement industry, especially with the advent of pro-steroids and precursor steroids.

- Intensify and update educational programs at the junior-high, senior-high, and collegiate levels on a yearly basis.

The exposure of the designer-steroid conspiracy should serve as a wake-up call to all coaches, administrators, parents, the governing bodies of high-school associations, the NCAA, professional sports, and state and federal lawmakers. There are athletes who are looking for external growth at the risk of internal peril, and they are getting plenty of help from people who could care less about their health and well-being. To all athletes, both young and old, remember: dying is not winning!

11

Testing Will Not Inhibit Development of Performance-Enhancing Drugs

Bruce Schneier

Bruce Schneier is a security technologist and commentator. His books include Applied Cryptography, Secrets and Lies, *and* Beyond Fear.

The use and detection of performance-enhancing drugs resembles an arms race. Because athletes are in a competitive relationship, and neither knows whether the other is using performance-enhancing drugs, both competitors will use drugs to ensure that neither has the advantage. Rigorous testing will not end this arms race. When new drugs are created, new tests must be created to detect them, which in turn leads to new hard-to-detect drugs. As long as it is economically feasible, sports authorities will continue to improve detection technology. Correspondingly, to remain competitive, athletes will continue to seek out new performance-enhancing drugs.

The big news in professional bicycle racing is that Floyd Landis maybe stripped of his [2006] Tour de France title because he tested positive for a banned performance-enhancing drug. [Landis was stripped of his win in 2007.] Sidestepping the issues of whether professional athletes should be allowed to take performance-enhancing drugs, how dangerous those drugs are, and what constitutes a performance-enhancing drug in the first place, I'd like to talk about the security and economic issues surrounding the issue of doping in professional sports.

Drug testing is a security issue. Various sports federations around the world do their best to detect illegal doping, and players do their best to evade the tests. It's a classic security arms race: Improvements in detection technologies lead to improvements in drug-detection evasion, which in turn spur the development of better detection capabilities. Right now, it seems that the drugs are winning; in places, these drug tests are described as "intelligence tests": If you can't get around them, you don't deserve to play.

The Doping Arms Race

But unlike many security arms races, the detectors have the ability to look into the past. [In 2005], a laboratory tested [cyclist] Lance Armstrong's urine and found traces of the banned substance EPO. What's interesting is that the urine sample tested wasn't from 2005; it was from 1999. Back then, there weren't any good tests for EPO in urine. Today there are, and the lab took a frozen urine sample (who knew that labs save urine samples from athletes?) and tested it. He was later cleared—the lab procedures were sloppy—but I don't think the real ramifications of the episode were ever well understood. Testing can go back in time.

The doping arms race will continue because of the incentives.

This has two major effects. One, doctors who develop new performance-enhancing drugs may know exactly what sorts of tests the anti-doping laboratories are going to run, and they can test their ability to evade drug detection beforehand. But they cannot know what sorts of tests will be developed in the future, and athletes cannot assume that just because a drug is undetectable today it will remain so years later.

Two, athletes accused of doping based on years-old urine samples have no way of defending themselves. They can't resubmit to testing; it's too late. If I were an athlete worried about these accusations, I would deposit my urine "in escrow" on a regular basis to give me some ability to contest an accusation.

The Prisoner's Dilemma

The doping arms race will continue because of the incentives. It's a classic prisoner's dilemma. Consider two competing athletes: Alice and Bob. Both Alice and Bob have to individually decide if they are going to take drugs or not.

Imagine Alice evaluating her two options:

"If Bob doesn't take any drugs," she thinks, "then it will be in my best interest to take them. They will give me a performance edge against Bob. I have a better chance of winning.

"Similarly, if Bob takes drugs, it's also in my interest to agree to take them. At least that way Bob won't have an advantage over me.

"So even though I have no control over what Bob chooses to do, taking drugs gives me the better outcome, regardless of his action."

As technology continues to improve, professional athletes will become more like deliberately designed racing cars.

Unfortunately, Bob goes through exactly the same analysis. As a result, they both take performance-enhancing drugs and neither has the advantage over the other. If they could just trust each other, they could refrain from taking the drugs and maintain the same non-advantage status—without any legal or physical danger. But competing athletes can't trust each other, and everyone feels he has to dope—and continues to search out newer and more undetectable drugs—in order to compete. And the arms race continues.

Some sports are more vigilant about drug detection than others. European bicycle racing is particularly vigilant; so are the Olympics. American professional sports are far more lenient, often trying to give the appearance of vigilance while still allowing athletes to use performance-enhancing drugs. They know that their fans want to see beefy linebackers, powerful sluggers and lightning-fast sprinters. So, with a wink and a nod, they only test for the easy stuff.

For example, look at baseball's current debate on human growth hormone: HGH. They have serious tests, and penalties, for steroid use, but everyone knows that players are now taking HGH because there is no urine test for it. There's a blood test in development, but it's still some time away from working. The way to stop HGH use is to take blood tests now and store them for future testing, but the players' union has refused to allow it and the baseball commissioner isn't pushing it.

In the end, doping is all about economics. Athletes will continue to dope because the prisoner's dilemma forces them to do so. Sports authorities will either improve their detection capabilities or continue to pretend to do so—depending on their fans and their revenues. And as technology continues to improve, professional athletes will become more like deliberately designed racing cars.

12

The Decision to Use Performance-Enhancing Drugs Should Be Personal

Jasmin Guénette

Jasmin Guénette, director of public relations at the Montreal Economic Institute, a libertarian, free-market think tank, is author of La Production Privée de la Sécurité [Private Production of Safety].

Although performance-enhancing drugs may be hazardous to health, the decision to use them should be left to the individual, not the state. Private companies and sports associations can prohibit the use of performance-enhancing drugs because people have the choice to accept or reject the rules. Statewide prohibition, however, makes the use of performance-enhancing drugs a social problem rather than an individual choice. Moreover, prohibition will not prevent the use of drugs. As long as people want to use performance-enhancing drugs, someone will produce and sell them.

The use of steroids today [as of 2006] is widespread in many professional as well as amateur sports. It goes without saying that in order to become a professional bodybuilder, steroid is a *must use* substance. Anyone denying this fact simply won't admit reality. Ivan Rodriguez, Barry Bonds and Jason Giambi are all steroid-fueled baseball players. If you look at Barry Bonds when he played with the Pittsburgh Pirates in

Jasmin Guénette, "In Defence of Steroids," *Le Québécois Libre (www.quebecois libre.org)*, no. 180, June 18, 2006. This article is reproduced with permission from the author.

the mid-80's compared to his 2001 season when he became the record man for home runs with the San Francisco Giants, you can clearly see he's juiced-up. Now, should baseball—or any other professional league—ban performance-enhancing drugs? The answer is yes, if they want to. But, should we be able to buy steroids at the local drug store? The answer is also yes.

If Major League Baseball (MLB) wants to ban steroids, it is completely entitled to do so. It's a private league. Its owners and players can agree or not on contracts that aim at banning drugs. Now, just like the National Hockey League and some other professional leagues in North America, MLB is the only league that can offer baseball players multi-million dollars contracts. One of the consequences of that superiority is that many of the players will then agree to rules that they would normally not agree to in the first place. But hey, nothing ties them to MLB if they are not happy.

This is the case with steroids. We can assume, with what we've seen in the past few years, that if pro-sports had permitted the use of drugs many athletes would not have hidden the truth about their consumption and we could then see what talent mixed with science can achieve in terms of performance. This is not going to happen soon though; the government is putting a lot of pressure on MLB "to clean up its act" and "Congress wants to impose uniform drug-testing and punishment standards on all sports leagues." [S.M. Oliva, "Pounding the Steroids Issue." *Mises Economics Blog*, November 28, 2005.]

Personal Choice

Private companies and associations should be able to define what rules will govern them without any intervention from politicians. A private association has no obligation to accept me if I don't agree to their rules, just as I should not be forced to join any associations I don't think are fit for me.

This logic should also prevail when it comes to the sale and use of steroids. If a group of people, let's say Bodybuilders and Co., think performance-enhancing drugs are OK, they should be left alone if they don't force anybody to follow their path. Sadly, this is not how things are done. Today, the debate about steroid use is widely dominated by morally superior do-gooders who believe it's not right for an athlete to use products that help him or her perform better.

Deciding to use or not to use steroids is exactly the same thing as asking yourself if you should go to the movies or stay home, eat a cheeseburger or a salad, have a beer or a glass of sparkling water. It is a matter of personal choice, a matter of preference. People look at the possible risks and at the possible benefits of taking drugs and then make a decision. For some the cost is too high. The risks involved may not be worth the price. Ken Caminiti, a former baseball superstar, admitted having taken steroids during his 1996 MVP (Most Valuable Player) season. He died in 2004. Even if his death is shrouded in mystery (some say heart attack, some say overdose), many are citing his case as a clear example of what happens when people use performance-enhancing drugs.

People are smart enough to make the best possible decisions ... and if some take too many steroids, it's their own personal problems, not a "social" problem.

I am not suggesting that people should take steroids or use other drugs. But just as I don't want other people choosing what's right for me, I don't want to choose what's right for others. This is what respect is all about; not forcing other people to think like you, to act like you and to obey laws simply because vote-seeking politicians and their allies think some products should be illegal.

Protecting People Against Themselves

One case often cited in the world of bodybuilding to justify making steroids illegal is that of Greg Valentino. This man was arrested for selling steroids at his gym. He was himself taking a lot of drugs to maintain his 27-inch arms. [See Chris Shugart, "The Most Hated Man in Bodybuilding - An Interview with Greg Valentino," *Testosterone Nation*, May 31, 2002.] A lot of people say this guy proves steroids should be illegal. But this is a one in a million case, and we should not merely look at this issue through this situation because it is the exception.

Even if prohibitionists are advocating "zero tolerance" when it comes to steroids and even if it is illegal today, this does not stop all the Valentinos of the world from taking the drugs they want to take. This is true today, and will be true tomorrow. Prohibition simply doesn't work because as long as some people are willing to pay for a product, a producer will be willing to make it available. Today cocaine is illegal, just like marijuana, heroin, and a lot of other substances. Is this enough to stop people from cultivating, transforming, distributing, selling, and taking drugs? We all know the answer.

It's a fact: the type of drugs used by Valentino can be hazardous to anyone's health. No doubt about it. But this fact is not enough to legitimize state intervention that aims to tell people what to do with their own lives. In a free world we must respect and tolerate, even if we don't understand, the fact that other people have different goals and dreams, and that they are willing to use tools we may regard as inappropriate in order to reach them.

Steroids should be legal even if they may cause health problem for some heavy users. People are smart enough to make the best possible decisions—as they see fit—for their own lives. And if some take too many steroids, it's their own personal problems, not a "social" problem.

13

Use of Performance-Enhancing Drugs Is a Problem Among Teens

Greg Schwab

Greg Schwab, principal at Mountlake Terrace High School, in Washington State, is a former steroid user who played football for the San Diego Chargers. Schwab, concerned about the impact of performance-enhancing drugs on young athletes, speaks to administrators, parents, and students about the drugs' negative effects.

The number of high school athletes using performance-enhancing drugs is growing. One reason for this increase is a shift in the focus of high school sports. Rather than teach the importance of teamwork and dedication, high school sports communities encourage athletes to excel at the highest possible level. Since pro athletes have reached the highest level, students want to emulate their behavior. Even if pros denounce their own use of steroids, high school athletes believe that they must use steroids to succeed.

D ietary supplements and performance-enhancing drug use among high school athletes is increasing at an alarming rate. Recent studies have shown as much [as] a 60% increase in steroid use among high school athletes. To better understand what has caused this increase, I would like to share with

Greg Schwab, "Testimony from Greg Schwab of Vancouver, Washington," *Hearing on Steroid Use in Professional Baseball and Anti-Doping Issues in Amateur Sports Before U.S. Senate Committee on Commerce, Science & Transportation,* June 18, 2002. Reproduced by permission of the author.

you some of the things I have observed in my 14 years as a teacher, coach, and school administrator. I will also draw on my insights as someone who has experienced steroid use first-hand for two and a half years as a college football player and an aspiring player in [the] National Football League.

Shifting Values

For whatever reason, the focus of high school athletics has shifted. No longer do we preach the values taught by participation in a team or individual sport, the values of competition, teamwork, dedication, and cooperation. These have been replaced by a new focus or value, simply to excel at the highest possible level. While you may be asking yourself, "what is so bad about wanting to excel at the highest level?" consider what many of these high school athletes are willing to do in order to excel. High school athletes use all sports supplements like protein powders, sports drinks, ephedrine, creatine, and androstenedione routinely today [as of 2002] as part of their training regimen. Any high school athlete can walk into a store or health club and purchase these dietary supplements [with] no questions asked. On several occasions I have had conversations with athletes I coached about these issues. Many times they have come to me to ask my advice about taking supplements to help them perform at their highest levels. I have always stressed healthier alternatives to these supplements, but for many the supplements are simply too easy to get. While I am no expert on this, I have always believed that dietary supplements can lead athletes to using performance-enhancing drugs like anabolic steroids.

The three-sport athlete no longer exists in most high schools today. They have been replaced by athletes who train year-round, honing their skills in one sport. Basketball teams play 60 games during the summer, plus a 25-game regular season. Baseball plays 50 games in fall leagues, in addition to the 25-game regular season schedule and the 50-game summer season schedule. As a coach, I expected my football players to commit countless hours in the weight room lifting, running, and working on fundamental skills. Add to this the proliferation of summer sports camps athletes and coaches can choose from, and it is no wonder that high school athletes have no time for any other activities they might be interested in. [M]any athletes feel they have to turn to supplements to have the strength to compete through the long schedules.

The Role Models

For many male high school athletes, pro athletes are major influences. They are the role models. They choose the jersey numbers of their favorite professional players. They emulate their training regimens. They emulate their style of play. And they are influenced by their drug use. When a professional athlete admits to using steroids, the message young athletes hear is not always the one that is intended. Young athletes often believe that steroid use by their role models gives them permission to use. That it is simply part of what one must do to become an elite athlete.

I hope you understand that supplement and steroid use among high school athletes is a growing problem that needs to be addressed.

Coaches, whether they intend to or not, put a great deal of pressure on their athletes. The demands and expectations of most high school programs rival many college programs. In a sport like football, where the emphasis is on getting bigger and stronger, coaches are constantly pressuring their athletes to gain more weight or to be able to lift more weight than they could a month ago. As a coach, I caught myself saying to my athletes the very things that made me feel the pressure to grow in size and strength beyond what my body was capable of naturally. Athletes grow to feel like no matter what they do, it is not going to be enough for their coaches. Couple this with the fact that athletes are by their very nature highly competitive, and it is easy to understand how and why they might turn to performance enhancing drugs like anabolic steroids.

One of the biggest challenges I faced as a coach was trying to effectively dissuade my athletes from using supplements and performance enhancing drugs. I have always been very open and honest with anyone who asks me about my use of steroids. I regularly shared with my athletes the effects that steroids had on me while I used them for two-and-a-half years during my career as a football player. My hope is that if I can relate to them on a personal level, they will be more likely to listen to me. Too often though, what they see is someone who used steroids and turned out fine. Instead of listening to me because I am being honest, they think that if nothing bad happened to me, then they will have the same experience. The problem is that there is too little information out there about the dangers of steroids. All adolescents hear is how much steroids will help them perform. We need to get the word out at every level and in every way that steroids are dangerous.

A Growing Problem

I cannot stress enough how easy it is to get supplements. I cannot stress enough how widespread use of supplements is among high school athletes. Drug stores, supermarkets, and health food stores all carry these supplements and they can be purchased by anyone. While I can only speak for the athletes I coached, I would say that at least 70% of them are using some kind of dietary supplement. Percentages of steroid use are much harder to predict, partly because steroid users simply do not talk about their use. It is not something that anyone would openly admit to. Based on my personal experience and the number of athletes I have worked with over the years, a conservative estimate would be between 5% and 10% of athletes I have coached used steroids.

I hope you understand that supplement and steroid use among high school athletes is a growing problem that needs to be addressed. I strongly encourage you to take the lead and help to curb this problem. Steroid precursors sold as dietary supplements need to be regulated; they need to be harder to get. I cannot stress enough what kind of impact supplement use has on young athletes. This, to me, seems to be the first step in helping to solve the larger issue of steroid use.

14

Testing Teen Athletes for Performance-Enhancing Drugs Is Mandatory

Robert Lipsyte

Robert Lipsyte is a journalist and author. He is best known for his youth sports novels such as Raiders Night. *Lipsyte's novels and commentary reflect his disillusionment with a culture that honors the winner more than the sport itself.*

Mandatory testing of high school athletes is necessary to protect teens from the hazards of using performance-enhancing drugs. Some teens who use these drugs have committed suicide. Follow-up studies on the young East German Olympic athletes who used performance-enhancing drugs reveal long-term reproductive and health problems. When experts recommend mandatory testing, however, high school sports communities deny that they have a problem and claim such testing would violate personal rights. While mandatory testing of high school athletes may be challenging and costly, the price of ignoring the problem could be even higher.

Saving David is going to be very expensive and difficult, especially since David, his parents, his football coach and his school want to keep David just the way he is, swollen with steroids and knocking down other boys on his way to victory.

Even as the investigation of the Bay Area Laboratory Co-Operative takes new turns and pro football and baseball play-

Robert Lipsyte, "Test Teen Athletes," *USA Today*, November 15, 2006. Copyright © 2006 Society for the Advancement of Education. Reproduced by permission.

ers have recently [as of 2006] been suspended for steroid use, the real intervention must be this: mandatory testing for high school football players. [After a track coach sent the U.S. Anti-Doping Agency (USADA) a syringe of a new designer steroid tetrahydrogestrinone or THG—in June 2003, federal and state authorities raided the offices of the Bay Area Laboratory Co-operative, run by sports nutritionist Victor Conte, whose clients included baseball player Barry Bonds and some U.S. Olympic track stars. The raid led to a February 2004 indictment of Conte and others, alleging conspiracy to give athletes illegal steroids and prescription drugs. Conte, Greg Anderson, personal trainer for Bonds, and Patrick Arnold, an Illinois chemist who synthesized the THG, received short prison sentences and home detention for their illegal activities.]

David is a real boy whose name has been changed for obvious legal reasons. He was a 17-year-old high school junior when he was referred [in the spring of 2006] to a Detroit-area psychiatrist, Michael Miletic, because of poor grades and depression. David's parents were upper-middle class and divorced, according to Miletic. David's haven was football, at which he excelled; he reveled in his father's pride at his success.

At first, Miletic thought treatment was going well. David's grades and depression were improving. Over the summer, he also grew physically, bigger muscles, better defined. He animatedly described his weight-lifting workouts to Miletic, a former Olympic heavyweight lifter.

Peer Pressure

Then David's face began to look bloated, and his arms and neck became splotched with acne, signs that he was taking steroids. He was nonchalant when Miletic confronted him. Everybody at his gym was doing it; it was his ticket to a college scholarship and maybe the pros. He was paying his $1,500 monthly bill for testosterone, steroid Deca-Durabolin and human-growth hormone with his dad's debit card.

David is playing high school football ... one of almost a million young men in a sport in which the stakes are spiraling upward as colleges and the pros scout for talent down to the middle-school level. More and more high school games are televised locally. ESPN and Fox Sports will nationally televise at least 21 games. NBC is airing a new drama, *Friday Night Lights*, based on the movie and bestseller about Texas high school football. MTV is offering *Two-a-Days*, a high school football reality show. Naming rights for high school stadiums in Texas routinely are sold for $1 million.

Miletic seethes with frustration. He tried to alert David's parents to the serious health consequences steroids could inflict on the growing adolescent brain and body. But they were in denial and brushed him off. David was furious at what he took to be Miletic's "betrayal." He quit treatment. Because David had turned 18 and was "protected" by patient confidentiality laws, Miletic had nowhere else to turn. He could go no further in alerting people who might stop David's drug use. This is no aberrant anecdote.

"The statistics from surveys show that in your average high school/middle school (grades 6 through 12) with a population of about 1,000—30 to 40 kids have cycled (taken more than just one shot) at least once with anabolic steroids," says Bruce Svare, professor of psychology and neuroscience at the State University of New York at Albany. "Steroids are cheap and easy to obtain over the Internet and in local gymnasiums and workout venues. Many bodybuilding websites have chat rooms and message boards where kids learn about steroids and how to use them. We don't have the luxury of sitting back and doing nothing."

Adults in Denial

Svare, who also heads the National Institute for Sports Reform, lectures on the subject. When he calls for mandatory testing, parents, communities and coaches first tell him they have no steroids problem; then they cite the high cost of testing and the violation of confidentiality and parental rights. "When they say that," Svare says, "I shoot back, 'But kids are dying from this. . . . What is the alternative? To see more kids die?"

There is anecdotal evidence of teens committing suicide after quitting steroids. Reports on the use of performance-enhancing drugs by the now-defunct East German Olympic machine contain dozens of examples of long-term reproductive and behavioral problems as well as elevated cancer risks and heart, liver and kidney damage. But long-term studies don't exist.

"It's an outrage," Miletic says, "that we spend all this time and energy moralizing about Barry Bonds and the Tour de France and nothing on finding out exactly what these drugs are doing to our kids. Is it because we don't want to know?"

Jim Thompson, executive director of Stanford University's non-profit Positive Coaching Alliance, says he is not opposed to random testing but thinks the cost makes it unrealistic as a blanket strategy. He would make it mandatory for teams appearing in nationally televised games and would add both education and counseling, for win-at-all-cost coaches as well as their players. "I've been struck by the importance of identity around this issue," he says. Teenagers are so passionate about making the team "that doing something 'irrational' like taking drugs with horrible long-term health effects seems like a reasonable thing to do."

It certainly seemed reasonable to David who, as his senior season progresses, is probably becoming a role model to young athletes who know exactly how he got to be so big and strong.

Meanwhile, Miletic observes uneasily from the sidelines. He says, "We have metal detectors in our schools. Police routinely pull kids over to search for alcohol and drugs. We have a potential national crisis here. Are we just going to sit back and watch it on TV?"

15

Testing Will Not Deter Teen Use of Performance-Enhancing Drugs

John E. Roberts

John E. Roberts is executive director of the Michigan High School Athletic Association.

Many high school athletes today are given too much attention, and in order to gain the spotlight, some seek the benefits of performance-enhancing drugs. Mandatory testing, however, will only draw more attention to these athletes. Moreover, the frequent and universal testing that would most effectively identify those using performance-enhancing drugs is too costly for most high school sports communities. These communities should spend their resources on strategies known to change attitudes and behavior, such as student-athlete-led programs that teach young athletes better ways to train.

I oppose drug testing of high school student-athletes; and contrary to Robert Lipsyte's [November 15, 2006] column in *USA Today*, this is a valid opinion of deeply involved and committed people that is neither a state of denial nor a do-nothing attitude.

One of the recurring themes of Mr. Lipsyte's writings over the years has been that too much importance is given to school sports and its participants. I agree, and I cringe at the increase in national travel, tournaments and telecasts of high school

John E. Roberts, "There's a Better Way than Testing," *MHSAA Bulletin*, December–January 2006–2007. Reproduced by permission.

events. Even high school athletes are being set apart from the crowd, and far too much attention is being lavished upon their temporal physical accomplishments.

Singling out high school athletes for drug testing only adds to this misguided notion that who they are and what they do somehow deserve special attention.

The only kind of drug testing that is effective as a deterrent to the use of performance-enhancing drugs is that which is the most sophisticated and is administered frequently and universally. However, the only kind of drug testing that is affordable at the school level—that which is occurring in New Jersey this year—is the most simple and administered to only a random few of the postseason tournament participants. This is barely a speed bump, hardly a deterrent. It does nothing to alter athletes' attitudes, nothing to change student behavior.

> *Drug testing for performance-enhancing drugs in school sports is a simplistic and ultimately ineffective approach to promoting either saner sports or healthier students.*

The Importance of Education

What can change attitudes and actions is education. And the kind of education that has proven to be most effective is the kind the Michigan High School Athletic Association is piloting and promoting in Michigan: the ATLAS and ATHENA programs. These are gender-specific programs, coordinated by trained school coaches, but actually led by student-athletes themselves. They provide alternatives to performance-enhancing drugs and demonstrate a better way to prepare for sports. The programs deconstruct advertisements that bombard youth with unhealthy messages and wrong choices.

ATLAS and ATHENA have proven to reduce use of performance-enhancing drugs and also to significantly reduce other risky behaviors and to increase healthier choices.

This is where our resources are needed. Not testing a few for performance-enhancing drugs, which is not even in the top ten of drug problems facing adolescents. But teaching many of our students to make better decisions for sports and ultimately for life.

Drug testing for performance-enhancing drugs in school sports is a simplistic and ultimately ineffective approach to promoting either saner sports or healthier students.

Organizations to Contact

The editors have compiled the following list of organizations concerned with the issues debated in this book. The descriptions are derived from materials provided by the organizations. All have publications or information available for interested readers. The list was compiled on the date of publication of the present volume; the information provided here may change. Be aware that many organizations take several weeks or longer to respond to inquiries, so allow as much time as possible.

Athletes Training & Learning to Avoid Steroids (ATLAS)
Oregon Health & Science University
3181 SW Sam Jackson Park Rd., CR110
Portland, OR   97201-3098
(503) 494-8051 • fax: (503) 494-1310
e-mail: hpsm@ohsu.edu
Web site: www.ohsu.edu/hpsm/atlas.html

ATLAS is a program designed by researchers at the Oregon Health & Science University to discourage the use of anabolic steroids among male high school athletes. Peer instructors and coaches administer the program to high school and community sports teams. ATLAS has been tested on over three thousand students and has been shown to significantly reduce steroid use.

Canadian Center for Ethics in Sports (CCES)
350-955 Green Valley Cr., Ottawa, ON   K2C 3V4 Canada
(613) 521-3340 • fax: (613) 521-3134
e-mail: info@cces.ca
Web site: www.cces.ca

CCES is an organization that promotes drug-free sports in Canada and in international competitions. Among its responsibilities is the administration of drug tests in Canadian athletic programs. Materials available on the Web site include educational materials, annual reports, and research papers such as *The Sport We Want Final Report* and *Ethical Challenges and Responsibilities Regarding Supplements.*

International Olympic Committee (IOC)
Chateau de Vidy, CH-1007, Lausanne
    Switzerland
fax: 011-41-21-621-6216
Web site: www.olympic.org

The IOC oversees the Olympic Games. Its antidoping code prohibits the use of steroids and other performance-enhancing drugs. The Web site provides information on the World Anti-Doping Agency, which was established under the initiative of the IOC, banned substances, and related matters.

National Center for Drug Free Sport
2537 Madison Ave., Kansas City, MO   64108
(816) 474-8655 • fax: (816) 502-9287
e-mail: info@drugfreesport.com
Web site: www.drugfreesport.com

The National Center for Drug Free Sport manages most aspects of the National Collegiate Athletic Association's (NCAA) drug-testing program. Additional resources provided by the center include the Dietary Supplement Resource Exchange Center and a speaker's bureau. The center publishes the quarterly magazine *Insight*, the current issue of which is available on its Web site. Also on its Web site are recent news articles on drugs in sports.

National Clearinghouse for Alcohol and Drug Information
P.O. Box 2345, Rockville, MD   20847-2345
(800) 729-6686 • fax: (301) 468-6433
Web site: www.health.org

The clearinghouse distributes publications of the National Institute on Drug Abuse, the U.S. Department of Health and Human Services, and other federal agencies. Among these publications are *Tips for Teens about Steroids* and *Anabolic Steroids: A Threat to Body and Mind.*

National Collegiate Athletic Association (NCAA)

700 W. Washington Street, Indianapolis, IN   46206-6222

(317) 917-6222 • fax: (317) 917-6888

Web site: www.ncaa.org

The NCAA oversees intercollegiate athletic programs and provides drug education and drug testing programs in partnership with the National Center for Drug Free Sport. Articles on steroids are frequently published in the NCAA's twice-monthly online newsletter, *NCAA News*.

National Strength and Conditioning Association

1885 Bob Johnson Dr., Colorado Springs, CO   80906

(719) 632-6722 • fax: (719) 632-6367

e-mail: nsca@nsca-lift.org

Web site: www.nsca-lift.org

Consisting of professionals from the sport science, athletic, health, and fitness industries, the association facilitates an exchange of ideas related to strength training and conditioning practices. It offers career certifications, educational texts and videos, and several publications, including the bimonthly journal *Strength and Conditioning*, the quarterly *Journal of Strength and Conditioning Research*, the monthly Web-based publication *NSCA's Performance Training Journal*, and the bimonthly newsletter *NSCA Bulletin*. Papers and position statements are available on the Web site, including *Anabolic-Androgenic Steroid Use by Athletes and Code of Ethics*.

United States Anti-Doping Agency (USADA)

1330 Quail Lake Loop, Suite 260

Colorado Springs, CO   80906-4651

(866) 601-2632 • fax: (719) 785-2001

e-mail: webmaster@usantidoping.org

Web site: www.usantidoping.org

The USADA manages the drug testing of U.S. Olympic, Pan Am Games, and Paralympic athletes and enforces sanctions against athletes who take banned substances. The agency also teaches athletes about the risks and ethics of steroid abuse. USADA issues annual reports and the quarterly newsletter *Spirit of Sport.* Its Web site provides access to Drug Reference Online, a database of currently banned drugs. The Web site's *Cheating Your Health* link provides resources on the health risks of performance-enhancing drugs and recent issues of *Spirit of Sport.*

United States Olympic Committee (USOC)
One Olympic Plaza, Colorado Springs, CO   80909
(719) 632-5551
e-mail: media@usoc.org
Web site: www.usoc.org

The USOC is a nonprofit private organization that coordinates all Olympic-related activity in the United States. It works with the International Olympic Committee and other organizations to discourage the use of steroids and other drugs in sports. Information on USOC programs can found on the Web site.

World Anti-Doping Agency (WADA)
800 Place Victoria, Suite 1700, PO Box 120
Montreal, Quebec   H4Z 1B7   Canada
(514) 904-9232 • fax: (514) 904-8650
e-mail: info@wada-ama.org
Web site: www.wada-ama.org

WADA is an independent international anti-doping agency that works with governments, athletes, international sports federations, and national and international Olympic commitees to coordinate a comprehensive drug-testing program. Its publications include annual reports and the magazine *Play True*, recent issues of which are available on its Web site. WADA's Web site also publishes a doping quiz, information on banned substances and drug-testing laboratories, and a searchable database.

Bibliography

Books

Michael S. Bahrke and Charles E. Yesalis, eds.
Performance-Enhancing Substances in Sport and Exercise. Champaign, IL: Human Kinetics, 2002.

Karen Bellenir, ed.
Fitness Information for Teens. Detroit, MI: Omnigraphics, 2004.

Howard Bryant
Juicing the Game: Drugs, Power, and the Fight for the Soul of Major League Baseball. New York: Viking, 2005.

Jose Canseco
Juiced: Wild Times, Rampant 'Roids, Smash Hits, and How Baseball Got Big. New York: Regan, 2005.

Mark Fainaru-Wada and Lance Williams
Game of Shadows: Barry Bonds, BALCO, and the Steroids Scandal that Rocked Professional Sports. New York: Gotham, 2006.

Harry Henderson
Drug Abuse. New York: Facts On File, 2005.

John Hoberman
Testosterone Dreams: Rejuvenation, Aphrodisia, Doping. Berkeley: University of California Press, 2005.

Barrie Houlihan, ed.
Sport and Society: A Student Introduction. Thousand Oaks, CA: Sage, 2003.

Pat Lenahan	*Anabolic Steroids and Other Performance-Enhancing Drugs.* New York: Taylor & Francis, 2003.
Suzanne LeVert	*The Facts about Steroids.* Tarrytown, NY: Benchmark, 2005.
John McCloskey and Julian Bailes	*When Winning Costs Too Much: Steroids, Supplements, and Scandal in Today's Sports.* Lanham, MD: Taylor Trade, 2005.
Andy Miah	*Genetically Modified Athletes: Biomedical Ethics, Gene Doping and Sport.* New York: Routledge, 2004.
David R. Mottram, ed.	*Drugs in Sport.* New York: Routledge, 2005.
Richard W. Pound	*Inside the Olympics: A Behind-the-Scenes Look at the Politics, the Scandals, and the Glory of the Games.* Etobicoke, ON: J. Wiley & Sons Canada, 2006.
Claudio Tamburrini and Torbjörn Tännsjö, eds.	*Genetic Technology and Sport: Ethical Questions.* New York: Routledge, 2005.
James D. Torr, ed.	*Sports and Athletes.* Farmington Hills, MI: Greenhaven, 2005.
Steven Ungerleider	*Faust's Gold: Inside the East German Doping Machine.* New York: Thomas Dunne/St. Martin's, 2001.
Marvin Zuckerman	*Sensation Seeking and Risky Behavior.* Washington, DC: American Psychological Association, 2007.

Periodicals

Nancy Armour | "Steroid's Problems Are Years Away," *Associated Press*, March 3, 2007.

Drake Bennett | "Are Steroids as Bad as We Think They Are?" *Boston Globe*, December 12, 2004.

Thomas Boswell | "Don't Make Bonds a Guilty Pleasure," *Washington Post*, March 12, 2007.

Danny Duncan Collum | "'I Yam What I Yam . . .' (. . . Except for Those Performance-Enhancing Drugs,)" *Sojourners*, March 2005.

Norman Fost | "Let the Doping Begin," *Seed*, February 21, 2006.

Issues & Controversies on File | "Update: Performance-Enhancing Substances," June 24, 2005.

Douglas Kern | "Our Asterisked Heroes," *New Atlantis*, Summer 2004.

Gwen Knapp | "Extreme Measures; Athletes Willing to Do Anything to Excel Are at Root of Problem," *San Francisco Chronicle*, July 23, 2006.

Tim Layden | "Outrunning the Past," *Sports Illustrated*, March 27, 2006.

Mark McClusky | "Nix the Ban on Sports Drugs," *Wired*, September 21, 2005.

New Scientist | "The Race Against Cheats Will Run On," February 11, 2006.

Timothy D.
Noakes

"Tainted Glory: Doping and Athletic Performance," *New England Journal of Medicine*, August 26, 2004.

Dan O'Neill

"Ambivalence Is the Fallout from Drug Use in Sports," *St. Louis Post-Dispatch*, March 4, 2007.

Michael Ormsbee
and Matt
Vukovich

"Performance-Enhancing Drugs: Who's Taking Them, and What Are the Benefits and Risks?" *IDEA Fitness Journal*, May 2005.

Ken Rosenthal

"End the Steroid Guilt by (Players) Association," *Sporting News*, December 13, 2004.

Ken Rosenthal

"Even with Testing Offenses Will Be Pumped Up," *Sporting News*, March 4, 2005.

Marissa Saltzman

"Chemical Edge: The Risks of Performance-Enhancing Drugs," *Odyssey*, May 2006.

Adam Thompson

"Is Baseball Drugs Ruling a Fourth-Amendment Foul?" *Wall Street Journal*, January 16, 2007.

Ben Walker

"Steroids Saved Baseball's Future," *Charleston Gazette* (West Virginia), July 22, 2006.

Childs Walker

"Preserving Image Is High Priority," *Baltimore Sun* (Maryland), October 9, 2006.

Matt Welch

"George Bush vs. Barry Bonds," *Reason*, December 8, 2004.

Jason Whitlock   "Players Pay a Price at Health's Expense," *Kansas City Star*, February 4, 2007.

Web Sites

MedLine Plus: Anabolic Steroids (www.nlm.nih.gov/ medlineplus/anabolicsteroids.html) Produced by the National Library of Medicine, this Web site provides information on the health risks of steroids and links to drug enforcement and anti-drug abuse organizations.

National Institute on Drug Abuse: Steroid Abuse Web Site (www.steroidabuse.org) A public education initiative of the National Institute on Drug Abuse (NIDA) and several partners, including the American College of Sports Medicine, the American Academy of Pediatrics, and the National College Athletic Association, this Web site provides information and articles that alert people, especially teenagers, about the dangers of anabolic steroids.

Steroid Law (www.steroidlaw.com) Run by criminal attorney and former bodybuilder Rick Collins, who believes that the health risks of steroids have been exaggerated, this Web site provides health and legal information to people curious about using steroids and advocates the reform of current steroid laws.

Index

Pressure
    on athletes to perform, 31–32
    peer, 83–84
    political, 58, 60
Prisoner's dilemma, 71–72
Privacy matters, 60
Proactive solutions, 67–68
Professional athletes
    mandatory testing of, 56–58
    penalties for, 21–23, 54–55
    as role models, 79
    use of performance-enhancing drugs by, 7–10, 11, 29–30, 50, 73–74
Professional sports
    anti-doping policies in, 13–15, 54–55
    as enhanced reality, 31–32
    integrity of, 58
    resistance to drug testing in, 14–15
    security issue of doping in, 70–72
    slow response to steroid use by, 13–15
    steroid scandals in, 7–10, 15–16, 54, 83
Professional Sports Integrity Act (2005), 56
Professional Sports Integrity and Accountability Act, 56
Pro-steroids, 66–67
Pyramiding, 66

R

Random drug testing, 14, 53
Reese, Charley, 33
Regulations
    federal proposals for, 55–58
    on Olympic sports, 52–53
    See also Anti-doping policies
Rhoden, Bill, 47

Roberts, William, 13, 20, 23
Robinson, Jackie, 8
Rodriguez, Ivan, 73
'roid rage, 17
Role models, 32, 58, 79
Romanowski, Bill, 50
Ruth, Babe, 8, 33, 35

S

Safran, Mark, 18, 21
Schneier, Bruce, 69–72
Selig, Bud, 58
Side effects
    adverse, 12, 12–13, 17, 24–28, 50
    from hGH, 30–31
Skin conditions, 26
Sosa, Sammy, 10, 15, 39
Spectator sports, 10
Sport Association Unions, 54
Sport doctors, 43, 50–51
Sports
    competitive advantage as part of, 37–40
    dangers of, 42
    debate over steroids in, 50–51
    as entertainment, 31–32
    obsession with winning in, 35–36
    reality vs. unreality in, 31–32
    role of, in American culture, 7–8
    rules in, 41–43
    spectator, 10
    See also High school sports; Professional sports
Sports heroes, 8–9, 29–30
Steroid precursors, 55, 66–67
Steroid scandals, in professional sports, 7–10, 15–16, 54, 83

Steroids
    addiction to, 28
    advances in, 14–15
    adverse side effects of, 12,
      12–13, 17, 24–28, 50
    behavior effects of, 27–28
    clinical benefits of, 17
    competitive advantage gained
      by, 39–40
    designer, 63–68
    education programs to pre-
      vent use of, 20
    in high schools, 66–67, 77–81
    increasing use of, 65–66
    introduction of, 12
    medical supervision, 50–51
    oral, 17, 26
    over-the-counter-pills, 66–67
    personal decision to use,
      73–76
    precursor, 66–67
    pressure to use, 29–32
    suicide and, 85
    techniques for taking, 66
    use of, 12–13
    ways to curb use of, 67–68
    See also Performance-
      enhancing drugs
Stevens, Ted, 61
Stimulants, 12
Strokes, 25
Student athletes. *See* High school
  athletes
Suicide, 82, 85
Sullum, Jacob, 45
Superman effect, 31–32
Supplements
    ease of getting, 80
    education about, 53–54
    over-the-counter, 66–67
    use of, among teens, 77–81
    See also Performance-
      enhancing drugs

T

Teen athletes. *See* High school
  athletes
Teenagers. *See* Adolescents
Testimony, leaking of, 38
Testing. *See* Drug testing
Testosterone
    androstenedione, 15
    designer steroids and, 63–68
    growth and, 25
    penalties for use of, 34
    performance gains from,
      46–47
    steroids and, 12
Tetrahydrogestrinone (THG)
    difficulty in detecting, 20, 64
    introduction of, 13–15
    newer versions, 83
    synthesizing of, 38
    testing for, 18
Thomson, Bobby, 39
Tour de France, 69

U

UCLA Olympic Analytical Labora-
  tory, 60
Undetectable substances, 15
Urinalysis drug tests, 51–52
U.S. Anti-Doping Agency
  (USADA), 53
    BALCO investigation by, 13–
      14, 37–38, 54–55, 82
    creation of, 13
    drug testing authority of,
      59–62
    procedures of, 34, 55
U.S. Boxing Commission, 55
U.S. Congress, legislation pro-
  posed by, 55–58, 74
U.S. Olympic Committee (USOC),
  52–53, 54, 61

V

Vainio, Martti, 19
Valentino, Greg, 76
Violent behavior, 27–28
Viral infections, 26

W

Wadler, Gary I., 17, 22
Winning, 35–36
World Anti-Doping Agency
(WADA), 13, 47, 52–54, 60–62

World Anti-Doping Agency
(WADA) Code, 22, 52–53

Y

Yesalis, Charles, 11, 17, 18
Young, Jerome, 50

Z

Zero tolerance, 76